READING, WRITING, AND LANGUAGE

READING, WRITING, AND LANGUAGE

A Practical Guide For Primary Teachers

Marlene J. McCracken
and
Robert A. McCracken

1979

Peguis Publishers Limited
Winnipeg, Canada
462 Hargrave Street
R3A 0X5

Canadian Cataloguing in Publication Data
McCracken, Marlene J., 1932-
Reading, writing, and language

Bibliography : p.
Includes index.
ISBN 0-919566-71-5

1. Reading (Primary)   2. Language arts
(Primary)   I. McCracken, Robert A., 1926-
II. Title.
LB1525.M23   372.4'1   C79-091030-6

Seventh Printing December 1985

Printed and bound in Canada

Contents

Foreword

Reading is Only the Tiger's Tail was published in 1972. In it we described a basic approach to teaching language skills. In the seven years since, we have worked with a great number of teachers in the western United States and Canada. *Reading, Writing, and Language* reflects this work.

There are new ideas in *Reading, Writing, and Language* but, more, there is a change in emphasis. It focuses on primary grades only. There is explication of basic ways of working with children. There is an emphasis upon thinking, writing and spelling, and chanting and singing. The ways explicated have been tried in many classrooms, and the descriptions in the book are final versions that worked well. However, they are not thought to be absolute or inviolable; they are good ways to use when learning the techniques.

We are aware that research in linguistics and psycholinguistics seems to support the techniques. However, we did not begin with research or theory. We began pragmatically, and changed or augmented pragmatically so that the techniques worked well with children. We did have one theoretical notion to guide us. We wanted children to understand *easily* the functions of language, and we never wanted children's attention so concentrated upon skills or technical bits that the functions were obscure.

We know that children will practise the technical skills of language (letter-sound relationships, handwriting of letters, copying words, pronouncing words orally, etc.) because the technical skills are interesting and children like to learn everything. However, we sense that children who learn skills without understanding their function may not, or may transfer poorly, the skills to reading and writing. Hence, communication and thought are present almost always, and skills grow out of function.

Reading, Writing, and Language is basic education. Basic education is teaching children to think and to communicate. Talking, listening, reading and writing are basic ways to communicate; but art, music, film, chanting, dance, drama, etc., are also basic ways to express ideas, and they are basic ways to interpret what has been learned. The teacher chooses a topic, a theme, a concept, and teaches seriously. She uses art, music, film, etc., to explore the topic with children. She provides many ways for learning and for expressing ideas. Of course, she includes talking, listening, reading and writing, but printed language is easier to learn when the concepts and content are rich both cognitively and affectively.

The arts provide the richness. The technical bits of written language are practised meaningfully if the content is rich. Basic reading and writing skills are taught because they are needed; there is no way, except teacher dereliction, to avoid basic skills when concepts and content are taught seriously. The more ways the teacher uses the more likely every child will understand the language fully and richly. When meaning is rich, the form can be learned, and it can be learned with ease.

Reading, Writing, and Language is not a program in the usual sense of the word. Children do not have to be fitted to the *program*. Nor does the teacher attempt to tailor a teaching program for each child. The *program* does not meet each child's needs. Rather the rich language environment directed toward all sensory modalities allows each child to select from the teaching and materials. Each child meets his own needs by taking what he can and what he needs to practise with the language effectively. To practise is an innate response of children. The teacher guides and demands so that the children practise effectively, but each child selects from the teaching "smorgasbord". Individual needs are met by providing children with a multitude of ways to practise; the key to effective individualization is in the practices through which children learn and in their practising until they have learned.

We would like to acknowledge that the ways of teaching described in *Reading, Writing, and Language* are not new. Ancient Roman works mention teaching writing and reading at the same time. The use of children's experiences as a base for language instruction was advocated more than 100 years ago. The *Shaker Abecedarius* of 1882 advocated singing and chanting as part of the basic school curriculum in language for beginners. Much of the methodology was part of teacher training in British Columbia in the 1910-20's when Marlene's mother, Winnifred Sheppard, was trained and taught.

In the past seven years we have had the good fortune to work with thousands of teachers. We are indebted to them for their faith in children, and the sharing of their classrooms and their successes. We wish to give thanks to all, and mention some by name for their continuous support:

Ethel Buchanan, Orin Cochrane, Janet Redgwell, A. W. Shalay and the teachers and librarians in Shaughnessy Park, William Whyte and Mulvey Schools in Winnipeg, Man.

The teachers, aides, and principals of Clear Lake and Mary Purcell Elementary Schools in Sedro-Woolley, WA, Roosevelt and Westview Elementary Schools in Burlington, WA, and Mountain View Primary School in Ferndale, WA.

Mary Ann Binford, Carol Campbell, Veronica Honiker, Mary Utrip, and teachers in Albuquerque, NM.

Frank T. Kennedy, Fred Kirkham and Olive Stewart, Coquitlam, B.C.

Eugenie Howard, Ventura County, CA; Patricia Horkan, San Mateo and Santa Barbara, CA; Barbara Evans, El Cajon, CA; Ruth Holland, Santa Clara, CA; Glenna Qualls, Soccorro, NM; Bill Palmer, Tacoma, WA; Helen Coe, Ames, IA; Kathy Carr, Cherokee, KS; Gary Heck, Lethbridge, Alta.; Gloria Mehrens, Seattle, WA; Nancy Underwood, Manchester, TN.

The teachers and principals of Maple, Roosevelt, and Wilson Elementary Schools, Tulare, CA.

The British Columbia Teachers' Federation, the Alberta Teachers' Association, and the California Reading Association.

Clara Pederson and Vito Perrone of the Center for Teaching and Learning, University of North Dakota; George Lamb and Theodore Mork of Western Washington University, M. Jerry Weiss of Jersey City State College; Blaine H. Moore of Brigham Young University; Lyman C. Hunt, Jr. of the University of Vermont; Raymond Duquette of the University of California, Bakersfield; Bill Martin, Jr. of Holt, Rinehart and Winston; and Susan M. Glazer of Rider College.

Lastly, for writing the introduction of this book, we give special thanks to John Downing of the University of Victoria.

Marlene and Robert McCracken

Bellingham, WA
January 1979

Introduction

The proposals presented by Marlene and Robert Mc-Cracken in this book are essentially practical. No theory is expressed. No research evidence is cited. But theory and research in the psychology of learning to read would support the McCrackens every step of the way in their program. Indeed, one can go further and state confidently that the McCrackens' highly practical program is more in line with the most advanced research and theory in this field than any other book of this nature that has been written to date.

The most valuable feature of *Reading, Writing, and Language* is its consistent concern with fitting reading instruction to the child's thought processes. Of course, there is no more efficient way to plan teaching methods, but unfortunately many educators have neglected to take the child's viewpoint on language into consideration. The care for this shown in the McCrackens' program should insure that children will immediately understand their instruction in reading, writing and spelling.

Some of the passages in this book that illustrate the McCrackens' deep concern for the child's thinking, reasoning, and problem solving in learning to read are these (*italics* have been added):

- *"A child must understand* that reading is getting the ideas of an author."
- "Kindergarten is an oral program to develop *thinking, sensitivity* to language, and oral *communication."*
- "Teach in such a way that *children realize* that they are learning."
- "The *child senses that his thoughts are worthwhile."*

- "The teacher is a model. What a teacher does during and after silent reading *defines reading for children.*"
- *"Children need to realize* that the symbols they write should be written in the same sequence in which the sounds they represent are said."
- *"Children need to be aware* that written English is spaced into words."
- "We should consider that *some children cannot understand what they are supposed to be learning,* and cannot make themselves learn skills for skills' sake. It is for the non-learners or poor learners particularly that the *emphasis upon ideas* is important. It is through the concentration upon ideas that *they realize what they need to learn in language,* and then practise until they learn."

All these quotations reflect the conclusions of the latest research on the psychology of learning to read that I have summarized in my book, *Reading and Reasoning* (Edinburgh: Chambers, 1979). Recent research in different languages from several countries around the world is pointing to a universal conclusion about reading instruction. Learning to read is a process of reasoning about language. Children must develop linguistic awareness about their own and other people's speech and listening behavior. They must rediscover for themselves those concepts that led our ancestors to invent written language. These concepts are: that language has a communication purpose; that this communication purpose can be fulfilled by writing visual symbols as well as by sounds; that speech can be analyzed into elements; that these speech elements then may be represented by written symbols. With an understanding of these basic concepts the child is ready to work hard at practising reading and writing the code *because he knows why he must do it.*

The McCrackens show their appreciation of this fundamental conclusion of modern research on the learning-to-read process in all the practical ideas that they have created for the children of the teachers and parents who will read this book. It is extremely valuable for reading instruction today that the conclusions of modern psychological theory and research have been put into practical form in this book by Robert and Marlene McCracken.

John Downing

Professor of Psychological Foundations in Education
University of Victoria,
Victoria, Canada

CHAPTER I

Learning Language

Reading, Writing, and Language describes ways of working with language in primary grades. We believe that language is such only if it has meaning. It has two functions: the first is to communicate; the second is to record thoughts. If we must label *Reading, Writing, and Language* we would call it a language-experience approach to teaching English.

CHILDREN MUST EXPERIENCE LANGUAGE TO LEARN IT

Children learn to talk without undue difficulty by listening to those around them. They learn because speech is full of meaning. Children, in some marvelous way, sort, classify, and sequence what they hear, and begin to talk, practising until they fairly well master speaking. Similarly, *children must experience written language if they are to learn it,* and the written language they experience must be fraught with meaning if they are to learn how to read and write. *Meaning* — the ideas, concepts, and content — is *foremost* in teaching children to use written language. Comprehension, concept building and thinking precede a child's acquisition of skills. It is through the meaning on a printed page that children can determine if they are using and acquiring skills of written language. When they understand the content, they can begin to understand the

1

bits and pieces, the letters, syllables, words and sentences.

Initially, the teacher works orally with children to develop ideas. She presents the ideas visually, in both picture and written form. Children work with the visual forms of language and gain an intuitive knowledge of the ways in which ideas may be written, and they sense the likenesses and differences between speech and print.

CHILDREN'S EXPERIENCES PROVOKE THOUGHT

Children's experiences are the raw material for thoughts. Children need all sorts of experiences and they need to attach language to them. They need to learn how to perceive, how to respond to their perceptions, and how to classify them. These perceptions may be classified and organized into four categories:

1. Likenesses and differences
2. Repeated patterns
3. Growth, change, and continuity
4. Interactions and interrelationships

Spelling may be organized this way. Spoken language may be organized this way. Most disciplined study is organized this way. One job in teaching is to make learning possible by teaching a child how to perceive the information that impinges upon his brain. A second is to help teach children how to classify and organize their perceptions. Art, music, dance, etc., are forms for recording and interpreting perceptions of the world. As the brain is filled with the oral language of perceptions, it directs the eye as it works with written language.

CHILDREN MUST UNDERSTAND THE FUNCTIONS OF LANGUAGE

The teacher's job is threefold. She must teach children how to read and write; she must demand that each child practises reading and writing until what has been taught is learned; she must teach in such a way that each one is able to discern the functions of language. A child must understand that reading is getting the ideas of an author.

When a child understands this, his attempts at learning to read are aimed at getting ideas, and in attempting to get ideas he learns how words appear in print, and he learns how to say words in response to the printed forms. If a child perceives that reading is only pronouncing words, he may never get meaning from the printed page.

COMMUNICATION SKILLS

The teaching begins with experiences, experiences which the children bring to the classroom and those which the teacher provides. Experiences provoke thoughts; thoughts provoke a need to communicate; communication requires language. Communication is a giving and getting of ideas. We give ideas primarily through talking and writing, and through art in all its forms — music, drama, dance, gesture and body movement. We get ideas through our senses, primarily by hearing or looking, by listening and reading. Writing requires spelling and spelling requires phonics. Diagrammatically, this approach may be drawn as follows:

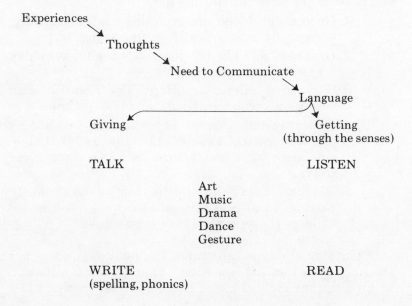

This scheme fits any content. If the teacher focuses upon content, all language skills become necessary and should be taught as needed.

PURPOSES OF *READING, WRITING, AND LANGUAGE*

There are five purposes:

1. To immerse children in oral and written language.
2. To have children use the language of literature as models for practising.
3. To require children to think.
4. To have children understand intuitively the functions of language.
5. To have children acquire ever-increasing skill in using language.

BASIC ACTIVITIES IN *READING, WRITING, AND LANGUAGE*

There are five basic activities, which occur every day and provide the structure for the day:

1. Recording: Ideas are recorded mathematically, artistically, scientifically, or linguistically.
2. Oral reading: The teacher reads orally every day for twenty minutes or more.
3. Sustained Silent Reading: The children and teacher all read silently for a period of time.
4. Chanting and singing: These are ways of having children learn the sound of language so that they can work with visual forms and can write more freely.
5. Themes: Every day the teacher works seriously with an idea. She may sustain work on a single concept for several days or even weeks.

The school day is integrated by themes. If a teacher seriously examines a theme with children, the examination will require the skillful use of language. The teacher must

teach spelling, capitalization, punctuation, etc., as they
become necessary, and since they are needed, the children
will sense their relevance. Relevance is not something the
teacher can impose, but she can teach so that each child
can sense the significance of classroom learnings.

THE DIRECTION OF LANGUAGE LEARNINGS

There is a sequence in which language skills are
taught. It is a sequence that is repeated throughout all
grades. In outline it is:

1. Oral development of ideas
   - discussion-home dialect
   - reading to — language of literature

2. Taking dictation (beginning levels only)

3. Independent writing:
   a. ideas
   b. word (idea) banks
   c. structures
   d. spelling

4. Reading familiar material

5. Reading unfamiliar material

All these steps will be developed later, but some comment is needed here.

Oral Development of Ideas

Almost every lesson begins with oral work to present
and develop ideas. We sometimes begin with a film, a
record, or a field experience, but the important first step
is the discussion that follows as the teacher teaches and
the children respond by expressing themselves orally.
Many children will speak in a home dialect, since this
is the only speech they possess, but over long periods of
time, extending to grade six and beyond, they acquire other

dialects.* During this oral period the teacher records many of the children's ideas on the chalk-board, on cards and on sentence strips.

The teacher reads to the children, and provides charts of poems, songs, and prose excerpts that the children chant to fill themselves with standard literary English. From this chanting and from the repeated hearing of longer stories children begin to read as part of step four, "reading familiar material." It is from this chanting and listening that children begin to acquire oral command of standard English.

Taking Dictation

Towards the end of kindergarten or the beginning of grade one the teacher provokes the children to make a capsule statement. Frequently, this will be as the caption for a picture that they have drawn to illustrate an idea developed during the oral period. The teacher writes *exactly* what the child says, taking no more than two sentences. This is a recording time, not a teaching time. The child reads it back immediately, and as a first step traces over the teacher's printing and, as a later step, copies directly underneath.

Through dictation children learn the similarities and differences between their speech and print. If the child dictates a "poor" response, the teacher knows that she must do more during the oral period. This is not *more* in the sense of extending the oral time on Monday, but *more* in continuing the oral work for weeks. Dictation is

---

*There is concern about dialect in some parts of the United States and Canada. There is concern that some children's dialects are considered substandard or less than acceptable. This issue is economic and political, it seems to us, rather than educational. A child will learn as many dialects as he experiences and practises. Most adults have several dialects, a kitchen dialect, a telephone dialect, and athletic field dialect, a thank-you note dialect, etc. Standard written English and standard spoken English may be thought of as two dialects. As such we feel that teaching children standard English is an educational responsibility of the public schools.

a relatively short-lived activity, covering two months or a little more. Children must be moved on to writing independently.

Independent Writing

Much of this book is devoted to independent writing. Independent writing does not occur automatically from dictation. Dictation helps children begin to understand the writing system of English, but children cannot be allowed to remain dependent upon the teacher for writing. If children are permitted to dictate too long, dictation becomes a crutch and a habit, and interferes with children moving into independent writing. Children need four things in order to write. They need ideas, words, and structure, and they need to know how to spell.

Children need help with ideas. They need to talk to sort out their ideas, to refine them. They need this oral work first because their first attempts at writing are not likely to be long, and without the oral work they are likely to record half thoughts, or the beginnings of thoughts, rather than a key sentence encapsulating a major idea. They need idea or word banks to help them remember the ideas developed in the oral work.

Grade two boys writing. The boy in the right rear is looking at the chalkboard where ideas have been previously recorded.

Children's writing frequently becomes a bulletin board for sharing and is changed at least every two weeks. (Grade 2, January)

Idea banks take three primary forms. These may be word lists brainstormed and compiled for use throughout the year. A list of family names such as father, mother, brother, uncle, grandmother, etc., on a chart is one type of idea bank. A list of monster words, compiled by brainstorming for words that describe monsters, words that tell how monsters move, phrases that tell where monsters might be, etc., is another type of idea bank that might be available only for the two months that children are working with monsters. Poems, song lyrics, chants, etc., on charts that hang in view within the room are another idea bank.

A poem on a chart may be a structure as well as an idea bank. A structure is anything that gives the child a form upon which to hang his ideas. Some structures are within the children because some song or poem or chant has been recited so often that it is part of the child.

For example, the song, *The Farmer in the Dell,* becomes a structure on which the child hangs his Hallowe'en ideas as he composes and writes, "The witch is in the house, the witch is in the house, boo, boo, she's scaring you, the witch is in the house." The same structure is available for "Santa's in his sleigh...." "The snow is falling down...." or "The daffodils are up...." Twenty or more structures are presented within this book. The simplest structures are the written repetition of the oral response to a simple question. "What do you like to eat?" yields the repeated oral response; I like＿＿＿＿＿＿＿＿＿＿＿＿＿＿, with the ending varying. *What can you do?* yields I can ＿＿＿＿＿＿＿. We call these frame sentences.

Spelling is discussed fully in chapter IV. Children must learn the basic alphabetic principles of spelling, and they must be taught how to spell. Spelling is a skill, not the learning of lists of words. Anyone reading this book upon hearing the name of a town in Africa for the first time can render it into written English. This is done by listening to and feeling for the sounds, and writing them in the sequence that they are said. To this we add whatever we know of spelling patterns. This may not be the correct way to spell the word, but it will be very close to it. It is this skill that children must learn, and then they can learn the standard spelling of English.

Reading the Familiar

Children read what they dictate. Children read what the teacher has recorded on the chalkboard or on word cards, sentence strips and charts. Children read the stories that the teacher has read to them — stories for which the concepts have been made familiar through the oral discussions. Children read what they have written, and they read what classmates have written. When they have trouble, the teacher moves back to the oral or the written to develop ideas further, or to spelling to develop word identification skill.

Sustained silent reading in kindergarten. (Most of the children were more interested in their books than they were in the photographer, who wasn't reading
— a clear violation of the basic rule of SSR.)

Reading the Unfamiliar

This last step is not an easy area to describe. It is common to think of reading level as determined by the child's ability to pronounce words. However, we believe that it is the ideas that determine whether a child can read a book, and, to a degree, whether he has in his brain the specific vocabulary of the content. Anyone reading this book is probably able to read fairly well in the field of education, but many readers will not have the background of understanding or the vocabulary to read easily in surgical procedures, aerodynamics, ham radio repair, home electrical repair, etc. The inability to read in these special areas is not caused by an inability to say the words; it is in not being able to bring enough ideas to the reading. As children read in *new* areas, they need to return to the oral teaching of step one to develop ideas.

Most teacher directed activities for chanting, singing, or developing ideas are done with the whole class. Note the cooking corner in the background, and the language structure in the pocket chart.

CHAPTER II

Organizing the Primary Day

A primary day may be organized in many ways, but it must provide *a time for teaching* and *a time for practising and learning.*

A TIME FOR TEACHING
How a teacher groups children for teaching is determined by the *purpose* of her teaching.

Teaching for thought or concept development is best done in total group because the potential interaction among 20-35 heads is greater than the interaction among 5-10 heads. The more ideas there are, the more possibilities for thinking, reacting and learning. Therefore, all activities which require sharing and expanding of thought are taught in total group situations. The authors realize that teaching a group of thirty primary children may be difficult, and they realize that to suggest teaching a large group may be out of vogue. However, children can learn to work in large groups if the teacher will teach and persevere through twenty to thirty lessons. The learning and benefits of communication within the large group cannot be found or duplicated in small group work.

Teaching for skill development usually is best handled in small groups or individually. Children who need instruction are grouped together for the lessons they need, and the teacher can monitor the small group closely enough to ensure successful learning.

A TIME FOR PRACTISE

Practising is best done individually or in small groups as children record individually their ideas or thoughts developed in the teaching session, as children work in Learning Centers, or as children read silently. Learning Centers are areas for learning concepts and practising skills taught by the teacher.

THE KINDERGARTEN PROGRAM

In the kindergarten year oral language is stressed. Children practise language orally. Seeing the printed word is primarily to help children sense the repetition of the language; it is not for formal word learning or phrase learning. Sustained silent reading is used. In sustained silent reading kindergarten children use books to review mentally the oral patterns that they have heard, to use the oral patterns as they recite to themselves many of the books, and to think about the ideas in books. Kindergarten is an oral language time that emphasizes thinking and concept development in such a way that children intuitively sense the patterns and power of their oral language. *The prerequisites to success in reading are being able to think, being able to sense the patterns of language and being able to express oneself orally with reasonable clarity.* Kindergarten is an oral program to develop thinking, sensitivity to language, and oral communication.

BEGINNING GRADE ONE

Beginning grade one is perhaps the most exciting time in a child's life. Most children come to grade one believing that they will learn to read and write, eager to begin. Some few are apprehensive, worried because they have already known failure personally or they have learned about school failures from older children.

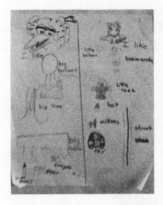

The kindergarten children brainstormed for things they liked. They chanted and then classified the ideas as big and little; some could be both. They each recorded their individual preferences on a sheet under *Big Bird* or *Little Bird* and the teacher took dictation to label the children's ideas. One child wrote his own sentence frame.

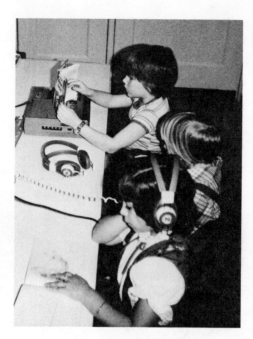

Kindergarten children listen to their favorite stories over and over again, following the pictures and the text.

The challenge to the first grade teacher is vital. She must meet the children's expectations, teaching them to read and write or she will lose them. If disappointed, the children will lose their interest and excitement and they will fail to learn. The teacher must teach so that learning is natural for every child. Her procedures and requirements must show all children that they can learn and that learning is joyful. Verbally assuring children that they can learn is not enough; nor is extrinsic reward. The teacher must teach in such a way that each child realizes that he is learning. *This is the key to successful teaching and learning. The teacher teaches in a way that enables each child to successfully practise what has been taught so that he learns.* Each lesson is followed by learning activities that suit both the interests and abilities of the children; the teacher, thus, provides a program that offers both challenge and security:

The program challenges each child to think, to discuss, and to share thoughts. *The program provides security* as each child senses that his thoughts are worthwhile, so worthwhile that his thoughts are used by the teacher and other children.

The program challenges each child to read. *The program provides security* by concentrating on understanding and meaning rather than saying words, and by using each child's own thoughts and language to initiate his learning to recognize written words.

The program challenges every child to record his best thoughts. *The program provides security* by teaching many ways to record thoughts so that every child can succeed immediately in at least one way.

The program challenges every child to work independently. *The program provides security* by teaching children how to work independently before expecting them to do so.

The first few weeks of grade one are most successfully handled through total group activities and instruction. The teacher gets to know her children, but, more importantly, the children get to know the teacher, and the room, the school environment, other pupils, and the types of activities peculiar to school before they are required to work independently or in small groups by themselves. The beginning weeks are the time when the children are taught how to do things, how to use materials, how to record, how to discuss, and how to behave. This is the time when the structure of the classroom becomes apparent. *This is the time when the child learns that he is free to learn in any way that suits him, but that he is not free not to learn, nor to deter others from learning.*

This is the time when expectations and procedures are clearly demonstrated so that each child will have the security of knowing what to do and how to do it when he begins to work without direct teacher guidance. *Children must know what to do and how to do activities before they can work independently.* Until children know how to work independently it is futile for a teacher to attempt small group or individual instruction because she will be interrupted incessantly with questions from frustrated children who want to learn and can't, or by children who have nothing to do. The physical activity of a young child is directly proportionate to his mental activity. The child who is engrossed in thinking and learning is relatively inert. The child who wants something to think about or something to learn about is moving around exploring and talking. Discipline problems are created by classroom structure that fails to teach children how to work before requiring them to work, and that fails to challenge the minds of children in their work.

THE PRIMARY GRADES

Reading, Writing, and Language describes the importance of thinking, of thoughts, of communication, and the two aspects of communication, the giving of thoughts, and the getting of thoughts. There are three major types of activities:

(a) activities to promote thought, to develop needs and desires to communicate, and the desire to record one's own thoughts;

(b) activities that teach the ways to record thoughts and the ways to practise thinking or learning;

(c) activities that begin with children's books as children listen to books read orally and as children read books themselves.

Through the *Reading, Writing, and Language* program children come to several understandings. These understandings are the goals or purposes of this program. They are not intended to be formally memorized and recited.

GOALS OF THE PROGRAM

1. Children are taught that their thoughts are important.
2. Children are taught that they can learn from the thoughts of others, particularly from their classmates and from authors.
3. Children are taught that their thoughts can be recorded in many ways.
4. Children are taught that writing is very much like talk printed down.
5. Children are taught to do their own writing even though their beginning attempts are imperfect.
6. Children are taught that they can read their own recorded thoughts, that they can read the recorded thoughts of others, and that others can read their recorded thoughts.
7. Children are filled with good literature so that the osmosis of both language and ideas occurs.
8. Children are taught to use the ideas of authors.
9. Children are taught to have empathy with characters.
10. Children are taught to think.
11. Children are taught to understand writing and reading.

Children taught this way take pride in their work, take pride in themselves, and take joy in communicating from their own writing and reading; they develop an independence of thinking that reflects enough conformity to communicate and sufficient independence to be interesting, and they develop an understanding of how language functions and how they function in learning language. One seven-year-old, second grade boy who had been taught this way for two years was directed, during an individual reading test, to *read a word list*. He replied in an inflected voice conveying incredulity, "Who would ever read a word list?" When asked to pronounce the words on the list he did, but he added before beginning, "Why would anyone ever *read* a word list!" A five-year-old boy finishing kindergarten was asked, "Can you read?" He replied, "I can read books, but I can't read any words yet." Both boys demonstrated that they had absorbed very important teachings, teachings that they had learned intuitively through a teaching program in which the goals, the teaching, and the learning activities were consistent and not hypocritical.

CHAPTER III

Hearing, Seeing, and Using Language

LANGUAGE PATTERNS

There are patterns in oral language that are almost replicated by written language, and there are patterns used almost exclusively for written language. The language patterns taught in kindergarten are those oral language patterns that are used in written form, and the majority of patterns taught in the primary grades are ones common to both oral and written language.

Books are a source of consistent language patterns. Authors can be our best teachers, since their writings can be repeated without change often enough for children to absorb the language. Children imitate and improvise from these patterns as they speak and write.

Books provide patterns of rhythm:

How do you say hello to a ghost,
Hello to a ghost, hello to a ghost?
How do you say hello to a ghost,
If you meet one in the hallway?

(How Do You Say Hello to a Ghost?)

Books provide patterns of idiom:

so smooth that. "The path was so smooth that he slid along it ooooh! ooooh! ooooh!" (*The Purple Snail*)

a long time ago. "In Bethlehem, a long time ago, people sometimes built their houses over caves in the stony hills." (*The Bethlehem Mouse*)

just alike. "They walked just alike. They talked just alike." (*Almost Just Alike*)

Books provide patterns of story structure:

Once there was a pretty little girl who lived with....
Once there were three billy goats that lived near....
Once there was a mother pig who had three little pigs....

...When the wolf awoke and tried to run away, the stones were so heavy that he fell over dead. And that was the end of him.

...As for the mean old troll, he hasn't been seen from that day to this.

...The little pig quickly covered the pot with a big lid, and that was the end of the mean old wolf.

The beginnings are similar, the middles have the similarity of impending tragedy, and the endings get rid of the evil, the bad.

The story structure may be cumulative:

This is the house that Bjorn built.

This is the tree with the nearby jail
that held the house that Bjorn built.

This is the squirrel with the bushy tail
that lived in the tree with the nearby jail
that held the house that Bjorn built.

(*This is the House that Bjorn Built*)

The story structure may be repetitive:

"Not I," said the cat.

"Not I," said the dog.

"Not I," said the pig.

"Then I will," said the little red hen, and she did.

Children need to hear patterns

Children need to hear these patterns time after time after time until they are familiar. This familiarity is evidenced when a child analyzes some part of a story, absorbs the pattern, and predicts what is to happen both in language and in plot. The teacher begins to read the story orally to the class. "Once..." and the child's lips join with the teacher in saying, "upon a time".

The teacher begins, "Do you live in a dog house?
No! No! No!
Dogs live in dog houses.
Do you live in a tree?"*

and the children respond "No! No! No!" because they have intuitively sensed the language pattern of the story. This sense of language patterns and story structures allows children to predict the exact language of a story as they anticipate the plot, listen to stories, and as they read stories.

(Where Do You Live?)

Children need to see patterns

Children need to see the printed patterns that they already recognize orally. Gradually they see, sense, and learn that writing is ideas printed down. Gradually they learn the conventions of written language, conventions rooted in the patterns of oral language.

Children need to use patterns

Children need to use these patterns in as many ways as possible. They can chant, dramatize, sing, dance, clap, improvise variations, etc., to make the patterns their own. The oral use comes first, and the practice is frequently in chorus rather than solo. The children eventually will use their practised oral patterns in writing, augmenting and varying as they learn to express their ideas; only a few children will begin written expression in kindergarten.

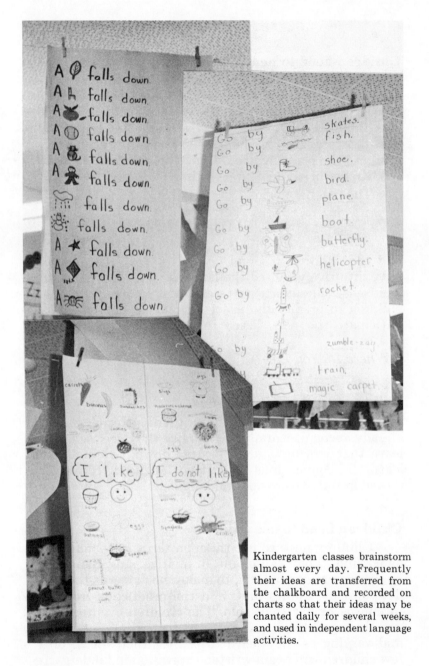

Kindergarten classes brainstorm almost every day. Frequently their ideas are transferred from the chalkboard and recorded on charts so that their ideas may be chanted daily for several weeks, and used in independent language activities.

Children sense language

This combination of hearing, seeing, and using language fills children with the sound and structure of the language, with the patterns that enable them to sense intuitively what they must do in writing and reading. Teachers must not fear repetition or drill. It is this sense of the familiar, created by the repeated use of language patterns and of individual books and poems over long periods of time, as much as four years, that gives children the security to read, and write, and think in their own way. Stories and poems do not suffer from repetition unless they were ill-chosen for their first presentations. Stories and poems gain a patina from use that enables each repetition to bring forth a series of responses more mature and better understood than the preceding ones. Words and language are dynamic, ever growing in each child or adult through usage. This dynamic quality keeps language untarnished as we repeat and repeat and repeat.

Much has been said about children sensing language. We are very conscious that this aspect of sensing may be a troublesome concept. We feel strongly that children intuitively sense language long before they can verbalize or generalize about what they are doing, and long before they can perform on somewhat isolated tests or test-like exercises that purport to measure language understandings. The teaching program, therefore, requires a teacher who has faith in her own judgment in choosing teaching activities to develop language, and a faith in the learning abilities of children as they participate in those activities.

BASIC TEACHING TECHNIQUES

Brainstorming

One basic technique is brainstorming. This is a total class activity. Usually the teacher is the recorder, and usually the responses are written on the chalkboard. The teacher records with words and pictures in kindergarten and beginning grade one, and by words, phrases, or sometimes sentences in higher grades.

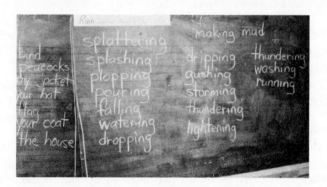

Rain may be brainstormed into classifications. All that remains is for the children to practise their ideas within some structure. This might be poetry, song, chant, or paragraph.

The teacher chooses an idea that she wishes to explore with the class. The idea may come from a line or an episode in a book. The teacher asks a question and then records answers as the children respond in turn. From the answers the teacher can tell:

1. What the children already know (and therefore what they need to be taught).
2. How the children express themselves (and therefore how much chanting, singing, talking, etc. may be needed before the children write or work independently).
3. What kinds of experiences the children have had (and therefore what additional experiences need to be planned).

For example, the teacher might ask:

1. "What is red?" and she might record in the following ways:

An 🍎 is red.   A 👕 is red.

An _etc._ is red.   A _etc._ is red.

🌷🌷🌷 are red.   Red 👞👞

Etc. are red.   Red _etc._

2. "What kind of witches do you know?" and she
   would record:
   > wicked witches
   > black witches
   > ugly witches
   > etc. witches
3. "What do your know about_____
   (Cinderella, the Pink Panther, snakes, etc.)?"
4. "What would you like to know about_____
   (Cinderella, the Pink Panther, snakes, etc.)?"

The teacher and children usually do three things with the ideas recorded:

1. They chant the responses in unison as they are recorded, and in several ways after they are recorded.
2. The teacher (and children) make copies of the ideas, transferring the language to cards and sentence strips. The information is then classified and reclassified as the children think about the information.
3. The teacher and children work with the language in the pocket chart, rearranging the ideas as they work with varying structures. The children then use the ideas within some structure(s) to practise working with written language.

The teacher *must* elicit at least one idea from each child when brainstorming. Forty or more ideas are a desired minimum for a class, and one hundred or more ensure creative, meaningful writing or other output from the pupils. Creativity in writing, drawing, drama, etc., comes from having an enormous number of ideas impinging upon the brain.

Anticipating and Predicting Language

Another basic technique is the deletion or omission of single words in sentences or paragraphs. This is similar to the filling in of blanks in workbooks or to the testing technique known as *cloze*. There is a difference, however, in that there is no single correct answer. The purpose of

These third grade children were brainstorming for ideas to complete an animal "cloze" as part of their work on an animal theme. The chalkboard is filled with ideas. The intensity of interest can be discerned from the pictures.

this exercise is to get children thinking and to get them to anticipate and predict the language that authors might use. For example, we might use the following sentence, and we would brainstorm for words that would fit into the blank spaces:

It was a_____night with the wind blowing_____
through the trees.

The teacher would record all answers for each blank, and then have the children check to see if the words recorded all make sense. Then the teacher would have the children check if random pairings of words made sense. They would discuss incongruities of meaning and why an author might choose a certain pairing of words; they would discuss what pairings of words would be appropriate for a mystery story, a Hallowe'en story, a romance, etc. They would discuss nuances of meaning that an author might be trying to convey by writing *black* night as opposed to *dark* night, etc.

Usually, this activity is completed with the oral group work. The children might use the sentence to begin a paragraph for a story in which they attempt to set a mood of mystery, scariness, serenity, etc. Merely writing the sentence one or more ways is not a thought-provoking task.

Classifying

Classifying was mentioned as one activity that grows from brainstorming. It is a basic activity in itself, and it is the basic activity of thinking and concept development. Classifying is putting things together because they are alike, or separating things because they are different; it is linking two or more ideas because they are similar and sorting out the ideas that are dissimilar.

The words that result from brainstorming are words that stand for ideas, as are phrases or sentences. It is important to recognize that we are working with ideas when we work with words. Children will record information from field trips, simple walks outside the school, or from books, films, etc. Children record observations, in words, phrases, and sometimes sentences. The teacher and the children record this information on cards or sentence strips. The ideas are then classified. A basic direction to the children is to *sort the cards into two piles according to some reason or rule,* and then to resort a different way, and then still another way. For example, we have the following words when brainstorming about what skunks can do:

skunks _____		
	spray	sleep
	walk	eat
	waddle	die
	stink	wander
	hurry	leap

Normally, forty or more ideas are needed for classifying to be effective, but ten words suffice for this illustration. These ideas may be classified in the following ways:

1. things seen vs. things not seen
2. locomotion vs. non-locomotion
3. things enjoyed vs. things disliked
4. everyday happenings vs. rare happenings
5. monosyllabic words vs. bisyllabic words
6. the past tense is regularly formed vs. irregularly formed

The first four are concerned with meaning; the last two with structure of the words. There are other classifications. The teacher may direct the children how to classify the words if she wants to teach a particular skill. Once children have realized what is expected of them in classifying ideas, they work in groups of four to six initially, and they work individually later as they practise classifying.

Chanting

Children need to work orally with standard English syntactical forms until they absorb these forms into normal speaking repertoire. Chanting a poem in chorus needs no explication except to say that children need to chant frequently, repetitively, and with expression that reflects a public performance standard.

Chanting from brainstorming needs explication. Chanting several times in one day is not enough. The teacher needs to practise from brainstorming in the same way that she would practise a poem. For example, the teacher and children have brainstormed and recorded in response to the question, "What is red?" She has recorded using the single frame, _____ is red, omitting the writing of the articles *a* or *an*. Each child has given at least one response and the class has chanted twenty or more times the responses on the chalkboard.

Each child selects a different idea from the chalkboard and illustrates it on a 3″ x 5″ card. Each child recites his picture within the frame sentence "(A ball) is red" and the class chants with him. The teacher puts a sentence strip in the pocket chart that says _____ is red, and each child places his picture in the blank as the class chants.

The teacher makes three or four charts, each containing the ideas of 6-8 children. The teacher may draw the pictures or she may have the children draw a second picture (identical insofar as possible) and paste them on the charts. The charts are chanted over and over again, and finally are hung in the Language Center for children to practise individually.

This winter bank has just begun and will have ideas added to it as children think more, read more, and listen to winter poems or stories.

The teacher may make a sentence strip book. Each child contributes his *red* idea on a sentence strip, drawing his idea. The sentence strips are punched and held together with a circular snap-ring, and the book is chanted several times on several successive days. The pages are shuffled from time to time so that no sequence is memorized.

The individual 3" x 5" card-pictures may be sorted (classified) in the pocket chart and the classifications chanted; or they may be affixed to masking tape and the resulting list hung and chanted.

The teacher may decide to use *a, an,* and *the* and possibly *my, some* or *all* and develop chants in the following patterns:

A _____ is red	Some _____ are red
An _____ is red	All _____ are red
The _____ is red	The _____ are red
My _____ is red	

The children will need to classify their ideas to discover which pictures fit into the various frames.

In all of this the children may chant their ideas two hundred times before the materials are put away or put into the Language Center for exclusively independent practise.

SUSTAINED SILENT READING*

Sustained silent reading differs from just silent reading because it is a period during which everyone in a classroom reads independently. Originally it was designed for grades two-three or above, implying that children had to read fairly well before they could read independently in silence. We no longer think that this is true.

We view SSR in two ways. Firstly, it is a time to practise what has been taught, a time for the students to drill themselves with language from a book. Secondly, SSR is a teaching time.

---

*We are indebted to Dr. Lyman C. Hunt, Jr. of the University of Vermont who devised the label, "Uninterrupted Sustained Silent Reading."

During sustained silent reading, everyone reads. The intensity of concentration is apparent in this photograph. (Grade 3)

Initiating SSR

There are six steps for initiating sustained silent reading. There is only one inviolable rule, however, *everyone reads*. The six steps are guides to facilitate the habit of silent reading.

1. Begin with the whole class.
2. Each child selects one book before the period officially begins.
3. Each child "knows" that he must read silently.
4. The teacher reads silently.
5. A cooking timer is set to signal the end of the SSR time.
6. No written or oral reports or recording of what has been read are required.

Some explication of these steps is needed. The *one book* rule is to provoke children into sustaining themselves with the content of a book as opposed to word calling their way through and then book swapping. Further, this rule fosters thoughtful choice, and prevents the restless child from using SSR as a book swapping time. The teacher must provide the following within the classroom if this rule is going to be enforced:

1. Lots of trade books
2. Catalogs
3. Class-made books
4. Lots of books which the teacher has read orally and discussed with the class, books that have been chanted, books that the class has worked with so that there are at least thirty familiar books for the child to choose from. Initially, this may mean two or more copies of favorite books.
5. Song books

Many kindergarten and grade one children think that the difference between oral and silent reading is just a matter that no one is supposed to be listening during silent reading. The teacher can suppress whispering and oral responses, but we think it is unwise, if only because the whispering and noise disappear without attention by grade two or three. The teacher should merely ignore the oral reading and attend to her own silent reading so seriously that minor distractions do not bother her.

The teacher must read honestly, usually from an adult book. The teacher must be indignant if someone interrupts her reading. This must be honest indignation. One way of summarizing the implementation of SSR is the teacher saying, "We'll all read and no one shall disturb me."

A cooking timer is used so that no one needs to be the clock watcher, and no child interrupts to ask if the time is up. For a start, the timer is set for 2-3 minutes and the time increased each day as long as each child sustains himself. Kindergarten classes should be able to work to ten minutes, and first grades 10-20. Some first grade teachers, and teachers of all-day kindergartens, use two periods a day, one in the morning and one in the afternoon. Second and third grade classes should be able to sustain thirty minutes, if they have had SSR in kindergarten and grade one.

Children need lots of practise to gain fluency. To somewhat master silent reading, we estimate that children need ten or more hours of practise for each hour of instruction. Not all silent reading practise need be under SSR conditions, but we should be able to justify taking a minimum of thirty minutes a day for this important activity.

Kindergarten and Beginning Grade One SSR

The teacher should realize that many children will select books and just look at the pictures. There is not much sustaining power in just looking at a book. Looking at a book and interpreting the pictures must be taught; looking at a book and remembering the language of the book requires that the book be read orally and that the ideas within the book be discussed so that children begin to realize that they should think far beyond the literal message of a book and far beyond the limited words within a book.

The teacher takes a large number of books and places them on a low table or on the floor. The children form around the books and the teacher samples several of the books, elicits conversation about the pictures and elicits responses to the text parts that she reads orally. She reads one or more of the books in their entirety. She explains the rules of sustained silent reading. Everyone is to choose one book; everyone is to read silently until the timer goes ding; everyone is to sustain himself by thinking about what the author has to say. The teacher sets the timer the first day for one or two minutes. DING!

The teacher pairs the children and allows them to share their books with a partner. The teacher should be a partner for one or two children each day. The teacher should share what she has read with all the children, but probably not during the first two weeks of initiating SSR.

The teacher should move toward longer sustained time quickly, but not so fast that children are unable to sustain themselves. In kindergarten, the ability of children to sustain themselves will depend directly upon the teacher's ability to introduce and discuss the books orally before the SSR period begins. Many kindergarten teachers who use SSR with great success spend forty-five minutes daily in book introduction and book discussion. The using of children's books does not always directly precede the SSR time, but all of the language and thinking activities that are part of the kindergarten day enhance sustained silent reading.

Many kindergarten teachers report that a few children, sometimes as many as one-third of a class, find it very difficult to sustain themselves because they want to hear their book read orally. We suggest that the teacher require the format of sustained silent reading as described, and that she use one or both of the following techniques:

1. When reading orally prior to sustained silent reading, make sure that the reluctant readers are handed one of the books that the teacher has read during the introduction period.
2. After four to eight minutes of sustained silent reading say, "If you have a story you want to hear, bring it to me and circle around. If you want to continue reading silently, do so." The teacher will

find that if she then reads orally in a quiet manner, many children will continue sustained silent reading for thirty minutes more, and those children who need the oral-aural part of language will get what they need, also.

In beginning grade one the procedures for initiating sustained silent reading are the same as in kindergarten. However, as first grade children begin to write their own class books and as they begin to write and recognize printed words, the introducing of books as books for sustained silent reading becomes less and less. Books are introduced and discussed as part of other activities, and these introductions replace the introductions of books just for SSR.

Teaching Through SSR

The teacher is a model. WHAT A TEACHER DOES DURING AND AFTER READING SILENTLY DEFINES READING FOR CHILDREN. Many children have never observed an adult reading, and many children who have seen adults reading silently have not realized what an adult does when doing so. The teacher can react orally to what she has read so that children begin to have hints about what they might do when they are reading silently. As a teacher reacts orally following SSR, she is teaching children how to read. We suggest that a teacher require nothing of children after sustained silent reading that she does not do herself willingly and naturally. This eliminates such practices as writing book reports, making lists of unknown words, filling in worksheets of any type, or taking tests.

Sometimes this permits the keeping of a reading log. Usually this means talking about some of the ideas encountered, and sometimes recording the more important ideas (note taking) for later use. Book sharing among groups of 6-8 pupils has become a popular ten minutes at the end of SSR, if the teacher has shared several of her books. Sometimes the sharing is within the whole group. Taking a particularly impressive idea, fact, or concept, chosen by any one of the groups and giving it serious study, occurs frequently if the teacher has done this from her own reading. Reading aloud to share a particularly exciting or well-written page or paragraph becomes routine if the teacher has done this from her own reading. Comparing and contrasting the concepts and content of books become routine if the teacher has done this from her own reading. Noting the significance of book titles becomes routine if the teacher has explained those book titles from her own reading that have hidden significance or metaphoric implications.

Sustained Silent Reading teaches several messages. Children perceive that:

1. The reading of books is important.
2. Reading is something anyone can do.
3. Reading is communicating with an author.
4. They are capable of sustained thought.
5. Books are meant to be read in large sections.
6. The teacher believes the pupils are comprehending because she doesn't bother to check.
7. The teacher trusts the children's judgment to decide when an idea in a book, when a phrase, word, or paragraph is well written, when something important has been read because the teacher expects pupils to share after SSR.

All seven are messages of trust and respect, a trust and respect that is returned many-fold as children learn by modeling from the teacher's behavior and respond after SSR to the books they have read.

CHAPTER IV

Independent Writing

A child needs four things in order to write independently: ideas, words, structures, and the ability to spell. Ideas are developed orally with the total group as the teacher reads to the class, shows films, arranges observations, etc., and discusses this input with the class. The words result from the recording of responses. Words are usually just lists of individual words, but sometimes they are in sentences or phrases.

SPELLING

A child must learn to spell if he is going to write fluently. He must become free of dependence upon copying words and develop an internal word bank, the words stored in his brain that he can write without consciously thinking. It is through spelling that the child comes to understand the alphabetic system of writing used for English. This understanding is necessary if the child is to use automatically spelling skill when writing, and phonics (word recognition skills) when reading. It is through the spelling program that the child learns all of the skills of independent word recognition.

The skill of spelling requires that the child learn and apply phonics. He must learn to spell his own speech. This spelling of one's own speech cannot be emphasized too much. We have observed many children who can spell the teacher's speech as she pronounces a word. We observe many children asking a teacher to pronounce a word several times for a spelling test. These children know the word, but they are unable to spell their own speech. Until a child can spell his own speech he cannot write independently. Most of the work that follows requires that the child think what he wants to say and that he do the pronouncing of the words as he learns how to spell. The teacher must keep her saying of words to a minimum.

PHONICS

Phonics is the tool of the writer. Phonics is taught to enable a child to spell. In order to spell, a child needs to understand three things:

1. The relationship between the sounds of speech and the symbols used to record speech sounds. To help children perceive this relationship, we first work to establish a child's learning a one-to-one relationship between the sounds he speaks and the letters he writes. Beginning learning should be what is easiest for the child. Consonants are taught first because one symbol frequently is represented by one letter in standard spelling, and because consonants are easier to learn than vowels. Consonants can be felt within the mouth because they stop the flow of air. Vowels, whether long or short, get lost within the mouth. They cannot be felt, and many vowel sounds are represented by two or more letters and the same vowel sound may be represented by ten or more spellings. For example: day, sleigh, date, wait, croquet, cafe, rein, or reign, etc.

2. Children need to realize that the symbols they write should be written in the same sequence in which the sounds they represent are said. We begin this learning by making the child aware of the sounds he says at the beginning of a word, then at the end of a word, and gradually those in the middle. This is not a strict sequence because the child works with

discerning the /t/ or the /m/ at the beginning of a word, at the end of a word, and sometimes in the middle of the word, before he works with a second, third or fourth consonant. (We use the slashes to indicate the sound represented by the letters *t* and *m*.) Nor is /t/ perfected. It is taught, worked with, and practised by the child, and then we move on to the next sound. Some children need to work with several sounds before they are able to discern what is expected; then they often learn many at once.

When the child has learned the one-to-one relationship and the sequencing of sounds, he will have grasped the alphabetic principle of our English writing system, and will be able to spell and write anything he wants to say. The spelling will not always be standard, correct spelling, but it will provide the child with a base on which to build.

3. The third step in learning to spell is the acquisition of spelling patterns. The English language is besieged with patterns. Most adults are still acquiring some of these. Spelling patterns should be taught and practised by the child. In all probability, patterns will need to be introduced and then reviewed for the child throughout the years of elementary school. We should begin with the simplest and most commonly used patterns and gradually proceed to the more difficult and rarely used. There is no correct sequence. We try to teach those patterns which are obviously missing in a child's writing.

A DIRECTION OF TEACHING PHONICS

Kindergarten

Kindergarten children need to be filled with language, the totality of language. They need to hear the fine language of good literature, they need to hear standard speech patterns and begin to use these patterns to describe their understanding of the world. They need to be filled with the various story patterns of the English language, to re-tell these stories in their own words, to dramatize their understandings of these stories, and to illustrate them in many different ways. Kindergarten children need to sing and chant every day. They need to HEAR language, SEE language, and USE language. We believe that a child comes to the act of reading with much more ease, joy, and success when the teacher has spent this kindergarten time filling him with language, and allowing or encouraging him to use that language in as many ways as possible. Kindergarten children need to gain an understanding of the similarities and differences between the spoken word and the printed word. There are two basic areas of understanding here.

1. Children need to be aware that written English is spaced into words. This is different from spoken language which is not broken between words. Many children, when beginning to learn to write, show that they have not grasped this convention of English writing as they join all their written words together in a stream of letters that resembles speech. Children need much practise in discerning "what a word is". Children confuse words, syllables and common sayings. For example, "How are you?" is often identified by children as *one* word, while "Hallowe'en" will be labeled *three* words. Most of this learning will come from work with written language on the board, in the pocket chart, and on sentence strips and word cards.

2. Young children need to work with *similarities* in words. They need much practise in recognizing that some words begin the same or end the same. Children need to repeat words after the teacher to help them to "feel" similarities in beginning or ending sounds. A child has to learn to spell his own speech and so we encourage children to "feel" sounds, rather than "hear" sounds. Spelling requires that a child hear likenesses; communicative speech requires attention to differences so that spelling is something new for children, and therefore, frequently, difficult.

The kindergarten program works first with language because language has meaning; the emphasis is upon content. Secondly, the kindergarten program works orally and visually to get children to recognize what a word is, and then to recognize the likenesses within words and the likenesses within sentences. This recognition of words, the patterns within words, and the patterns within sentences continues into the first grade. What might be termed formal phonics begins in grade one.

Grades One Through Three

Phonics instruction begins almost with day one in grade one, and continues within the spelling program as a daily activity. It begins as somewhat of an isolated skill lesson, but within a few weeks it is being practised within the writing of messages, and is not isolated from meaning because children quickly sense the reason for spelling.

We consider phonics a spelling skill used when writing, so we begin phonics by beginning spelling and writing. We teach the children five or six consonants. Simultaneously we teach:

1. The name of the letter.
2. The sound the letter represents.
3. The way the letter is written.
4. The way the phoneme is made within the mouth, the way it feels.

We have taught *m, b, f, s,* and *t* successfully as the first five. These consonants are used frequently and they are made quite differently within the mouth. Except for these two guides, the selection is arbitrary.

It should be mentioned that we can discern no "right" way to teach phonics; there seems to be no one right way. We are aware of the incorrectness of isolating consonant sounds. We are aware that it cannot be done, but we are also aware of the dangers of not doing so, and the problems encountered if all consonant sounds are combined with vowel sounds in order to maintain correctness. The isolation of a sound in the beginning teaching is a momentary device to get children to hear and feel the consonants within spoken language. The sounds are used immediately within words and are practised thereafter as parts of words that a child is writing in a message.

Children are provided with small chalkboards, approximately 12″ x 18″, on which they learn to write the letter as they say its name and its sound. This is the first step in teaching the alphabetic principle, and *the first step in developing the skill of spelling,* getting children to understand that if they hear or feel a sound when they say a word that the sound is represented by a letter. Initially a one-sound one-letter relationship is maintained to make it easy for the child to sense the nature of alphabetic spelling.

The second step in the skill of spelling is developing the understanding that spelling requires the sequencing of the sounds within a word. To begin this skill the teacher has the children draw two short lines on their chalkboards:

The teacher dictates a word. THE CHILDREN REPEAT THE WORD. The children must learn to spell their own speech, so the teacher, in teaching spelling, must say each word only once for children. Each word that the teacher dicates either begins or ends with an /m/. The children are taught to write *m* in the first space if they feel or hear an /m/ at the beginning, or to write an *m* in the last space if they feel an /m/ at the end. The teacher dictates 8 to 10 words on the first day, 8 to 10 different words on the second day, and 8 to 10 different words on the third day. The teacher may hold up pictures, ask the children to identify the pictures and to determine if they hear /m/. This entirely eliminates the teacher's saying of the word.

Each new letter is developed in the same way, but as new sounds are added, both the old and the new sounds are practised daily on the chalkboards. The teacher will usually dictate monosyllabic words, but a sprinkling of polysyllabic words begins the notion that children can spell big words, too, and begins the notion that big words are no harder to spell than little words. Once the teacher has introduced five consonants, a matter of two to four weeks, all five consonants are practised every day by dictating such words as *boat, seem, foam, might, surf, moss, team,* and *fib*. Once children have the two line notion and the beginning and ending concept fairly well learned, the teacher eliminates the two lines and challenges the pupils to listen for /m/, /b/, /f/, /s/, or /t/ in words like *stab, blast, fast, staff, stuff, bats, bets, must, muffs,* etc., having the children write three letters in sequence. The teacher should not be surprised if a few children begin to add correct letters such as the *l* in *blast* that have not been taught. Children do this once they have discerned the alphabetic principle and the fact that most letters have their sounds within their names. In doing this combined dictation children are practising and reviewing all the letters that have been taught and are thereby learning the sound-symbol relationships and the sequencing of letter sounds.

The adding of a vowel cannot be postponed much longer so we teach short *a* in initial position following the same steps used for teaching a consonant, except that short /a/ does not exist in final position. We dictate *am, at, ask, aspirin,* etc. We move almost immediately into medial position and dictate many monosyllabic words which they can now write completely, *fat, bat, sat, tat, mat, sam, tam, fast, mast, aft, stab,* and words like *staff* in which the child spells *staf*. Consonant blends are not mentioned as blends; they are merely taught as sound-sequences. We find that children handle them quite naturally if the teacher says a word once, has the children repeat the word, and then asks the children what sound they feel first (each child says the word as often as necessary to write the first letter), what sound they feel next (again saying the word as often as necessary to write the second letter), what sound they feel next, etc. If the child writes *sb* when trying to write *stab,* he is merely told that he left something out of the middle, and that he should say it again and listen. If he writes *sab,* he is told he left something out, etc. If he writes *satb,* he is told that he has the right letters but that something is out of order, and he is led to correct his sequencing. An integral part of teaching spelling is the correcting of mistakes as they occur, so that mistakes are not practised.

With the introduction of the first short vowel, the children's writing on the chalkboards takes on a different form. The children are taught to roughly bisect their chalkboards into four equal rectangles with their chalk.

The teacher dictates four words, saying each word once, and making sure that the child has recorded the word as correctly as can be demanded. To erase the words, one child is asked to read one of the words, and all the children find the word on their chalkboards and erase it; then a second child reads one of the remaining three words orally and all erase it, etc., so that children get practise in writing, spelling, and finally word identification.

Additional consonants and short vowels are added in the same way. Long vowels are introduced differently and treated as spelling patterns. The teaching of spelling is described in this book as a somewhat isolated subject. However, spelling is a skill for writing as part of a communication program in which children are expected to write at least one message every day. Children are expected to write as independently as possible.

If children are taught to spell and if they are required to write everyday, they learn to express themselves fluently and in considerable length. Some pupils find spelling very easy and make few errors; others find it hard, but they write just as extensively and their messages are equally interesting.

The following paper is typical in length and in the kinds of spelling errors made in grade one after five to six months of teaching. It is from the grade one Follow-Through class taught by Mrs. Jan Mahaffie in Clear Lake Elementary School, Clear Lake, Washington. Clear Lake is part of the Sedro-Woolley School District and is a participant in the Washington Triad Follow-Through Program sponsored through the Center for Teaching and Learning, University of North Dakota. The paper is from a child labeled as disadvantaged according to Federal guidelines of poverty. The writing is in response to oral work within the theme *Myself,* as children have discussed what different parts of their body can do. The sample is one day's writing, before any spelling correction (see practise p.p. 52-55). The italics are ours to indicate the misspellings.

My legs can *cik* a ball and my legs can do a *daes*.

My legs can walk me to the store

My legs can *duve* a *cor* and spot the base

My legs can run home and play with me

My legs can *wolk* me home and play out *baek*

My legs can *jupm rop* and hop

My hands can do some house *wrok*

My hands can *pic* flowers and pretty flowers *to*

My hands can do pretty *patning*

My hands can *bons* a ball and *rit*

My hands can pat a *god* and

My hands can play with my *god*.

The child has written twelve sentences using a total of 101 running words. He spaced between words consistently, indicating that he knows what a word is. He has spelled 85 of the running words correctly. He can read his own writing as can any adult with a little practise. The errors are of reasonably good quality.

Kick spelled *cik* indicates that the use of *c* and *k* is not yet learned as /k/ usually being *k* before *i,* and the *k* for *ck* is a spelling pattern not yet known. Neither of these spelling principles or patterns had been taught, and it is unlikely that they will be taught before grade two. *Daes* for *dance* is more worrisome because the /n/ is not represented at all. The two vowels *ae* in dance and later in back (baek) are a little more worrisome. We would prefer *das* or *bak* as a better quality error. The *ae* may have occurred because the child has unconsciously noted vowel digraphs in books that he has read; it may be that someone has corrected his spelling so that he now adds letters in trying to be correct without understanding anything about spelling patterns. *Jupm, patning,* and *god* (jump, painting, and dog) all indicate that the child has not mastered the sequencing of sound. These errors should be corrected as the teacher circulates and as the children write or as the children read their writing to the teacher. *Rit, pic, bons, rop,* and *cor* (write, pick, bounce, rope and car) are good quality errors and indicate that the child is practising as much as he has been taught. These errors would not be corrected at this time. They would be the basis for later lessons in spelling. Despite these errors the child has demonstrated that he has a reasonable grasp of the alphabetic principle. He is 84% correct in his spelling of the running words.

Teaching Spelling Patterns

Once children have demonstrated by their independent writing that they have sensed the alphabetic principle, they are ready to learn some of the common spelling patterns of written English. We begin with any simple one that seems to be interfering with standard spelling and move on to more sophisticated patterns in grades two, three, four and up. The use of the letter *y* to represent long /e/ (or short /i/) on the end of words such as candy, milky, silky, etc., might be a first one. The use of *s* to represent both /s/ and /z/ on the end of words to make them plural is one of the first taught.

Spelling dictation in grade two. Eight words, two sets of four, are dictated followed by a sentence using two or more of the words.

Five doozers hang in this second
grade classroom, the words are
printed on both sides of the cards.
There are five similar sets hanging
in this classroom so that they are
easily seen from anywhere in the
room. (p. 54).

Long vowels are taught as spelling patterns with children learning the most common forms. They learn that meaning affects spelling so that long vowel patterns just have to be looked up and learned. Common patterns such as *tion* are taught and practised in grades three and above. They are taught and practised by the teacher dictating eight words a day, four at a time on a chalkboard as noted previously. (We keep emphasizing the chalkboards; we see greater success when the chalkboard work is maintained for dictation, even though the children are working freely with pencil or pen upon paper.) The teacher dictates a different set of eight *tion* words each day for ten days, and then the children search as they read for /shun/ not spelled *tion*. They work together to note any spelling rule that they might form to determine when to use tion, sion, cean, etc. If they can discern no rule, they revert to the generalization that /shun/ is most frequently *tion,* but if they want to be sure, they either have to know or look it up.

In dictating *tion* words the teacher might use:

notion	motion	transportation
potion	mention	section
notation	demonstration	plantation
promotion	formation	meditation
lotion	information	reflection
premonition	rotation	correction
election	explanation	sensation
prediction	location	condensation
		etc.

Obviously, while the children are learning *tion* they are practising syllabic spelling, the letter-sound relationships, and the sequencing of sounds that they have previously learned.

Practise

The key to a child's understanding and learning is his ability to apply what he has been taught. To learn to spell, a child writes daily because he has something to record that he wants to remember or because he has something he wants to say. He writes sentences and stories independently and applies his spelling abilities in a meaningful context. When a child writes independently, he spells as well as he is able to. This poses the problem of *what is correct spelling*.

Spelling is perhaps the only skill area in which we routinely expect a child to perform instantly with perfection at levels well beyond what he has been taught. We accept a child's first baby talk; we expect a child to fall when he learns to walk; we teach a child to add sums to ten and never consider requiring him to do two column addition or division until he has practised simple addition to the point of mastery and then been taught some more. For some reason, we expect a child's first spelling to be correct, and we expect his first writing to be spelled correctly. If a child is to learn to spell (not just learn to write words correctly) then he must be allowed to practise what he has been taught, and we must demand and accept spelling that is as correct as can be expected as the child writes independently.

A grade one child wants to write *We went on a picnic and it was a gorgeous day*. He spells gorgeous, *grjs*. From the sentence it is perfectly clear that he is saying gorgeous. He has spelled it marvelously well for grade one, if he had not been taught that every syllable requires a vowel. If this has been taught, we would demand at least a *grjus*, and possibly *gorjus*, but the *r* sound requires special teaching all its own as a spelling pattern. In writing *grjs* the child has spelled all the sounds that he has been taught and he has sequenced them properly. He is practising what he has been taught. We must ask the question *is the child practising what he has been taught?* If the answer is *yes*, then there is nothing to correct now.

The way a child spells reflects two things. It reflects what he has been taught and learned, and what he now or still needs to learn. For example, if this same first grade child wrote that they had a race at the picnic and *"I ran fats"*, the teacher would tell the child he had made a mistake, and if the child needed help in finding the spelling error, the teacher helps him, or finally just tells him, that *fast* was spelled incorrectly. The child would correct *fast* as immediately as possible.

If a grade five child wrote, *there are nine posishuns on a baseball team,* he is either saying, "please teach me how to spell /shun/" or he needs to be reminded how to spell it. Judicious nagging is needed to develop good spelling habits. A child must practise what he has been taught, and teachers must look at misspellings and decide what needs to be taught next.

A child who writes *hope, cape, came,* and *tune* without the final *e* needs some teaching and directed practise with some long vowel patterns. The child who spells *grjs, hsptl, mtrskl* is ready for some work with vowels. The child who spells *winde, cande,* and *fune* needs to be taught about the use of the letter *y* to represent long /e/ at the end of words. There is no particular order to the teachings. The teacher chooses an obvious error, teaches it to several children who seem to need it, judiciously nags them in their writing, and moves on to the next spelling need when this one has been fairly well learned. Thereafter, she demands correct spelling of that pattern.

In writing or in speaking there is a small core of words that are used over and over again. A few are phonetically regular, such as *and, he, it,* and they need no special attention. Most of these frequently used words, however, are not spelled as they sound. It is impossible to write without such words as *is, was, does, were, they, because, why, of, the,* etc. A child will use these words three or four hundred times during a school year if he writes every day. He cannot be allowed to practise misspelling a word for two or three years just because the spelling pattern has not yet been taught. The third grader who has been allowed to write *thay* for more than two years will have learned the misspelling so automatically that almost no amount of nagging will unlearn it. For this reason we begin a doozer list in grade one as soon as independent writing begins. We choose five "doozers", print them in large letters on cards and attach them to a doozer chart or board. The chart is in a conspicuous place in the classroom, and the child refers to the chart as often as necessary in learning to spell them correctly. A misspelled doozer is always corrected as soon as possible. We find that teachers and children can remember up to five doozers at one time. When no one in the class has misspelled a doozer for 2-3 weeks, it is replaced by another.

In conclusion, spelling is a skill that develops gradually as a result of teaching and constant practise. As with other skills we should begin teaching simply and allow and demand that children practise as well as they know how. As children show us that they are able to apply what has been taught, we teach more and more sophisticated principles and patterns, demanding that children continue to practise what they already know and have been taught, until they have learned how to spell.

The two current practices of most schools, (1) the teaching of spelling lists and (2) the demand for perfect spelling (or even worse, never correcting spelling) in written work seem to be detrimental when children are developing their ability to spell.

STRUCTURES

Frame Sentences

The simplest structures are what we call frame sentences. They are merely standard sentence patterns of oral English, and we use them to elicit thinking and to make the recording of ideas possible for five and six-year old children. Usually we restrict the use of frame sentences to late kindergarten and grade one. Frame sentences are a marvelous way to begin children in writing, but they can become very constricting if children are allowed to be too dependent upon them.

Frame sentences are the responses to simple questions and getting a complete sentence as the answer. For example:

The teacher asks	The frame response
What can you see?	I can see (a, an, the) _____ .
What can you do?	I can _____ .
What goes up?	A _____ goes up.
What can your legs do?	My legs can _____ .

The teacher asks such a question, and then records the individual responses on the chalkboard. The first time this is done, the teacher records the children's names as part of the response. For example:

John can see a tree.

Mary can see a dog.

Mildred can see a house, etc.

The teacher has the whole class chant back the responses several times. She may draw pictures for what is seen, keeping the children involved as she draws, by asking questions that keep the children giving additional perceptions of what to draw to make the tree look more like a tree. The teacher may draw just the trunk and then ask, "What else do I need?"

The teacher moves by the second or third day to writing *I* in place of the pupils' names, and children begin to record their perceptions and ideas with frame sentences. She does this in somewhat the following manner. We find individual chalkboards indispensable in doing this. The teacher asks:

What did you see on the way to school? She elicits the patterned responses:

I saw a dog.

I saw a tree.

I saw two motorcycles, etc.,

until she has at least one response from each child recorded in words on the chalkboard. She chants the responses with the children.

Each child is now given a chalkboard and the teacher writes *I* on her chalkboard, telling the children how to make *I* if necessary, and each child writes *I* on his or her chalkboard. She has the children practise *I* several times, and then teaches *saw* and has the children write *saw* several times. (For those children who have difficulty, the teacher provides an individual word card which they place on their chalkboards and they copy directly underneath.)

Next, each child decides which thing that he wants to record. If it is already on the chalkboard, the teacher makes the child point to it, and she then gives him that

word on an individual card. (Many children may be able
to locate and copy the word directly from the chalkboard,
but use of the cards assures success and is best when the
teacher does not know her pupils too well. Further, the
word cards may be used for a classification exercise as
children sort their ideas into categories.) Each child is
given a sheet of paper and writes his name on it, draws
a picture to illustrate himself seeing something on the way
to school, and writes the frame sentence as a caption. The
children share their papers with each other as they work;
the teacher circulates as they work giving assistance if
necessary, and supplying any child with the full sentence
on a strip, *I saw a dog,* if he seems unable to understand
and write a sequenced sentence.

When all the papers are finished each child reads his
sentence to the teacher, then the whole class forms and
the teacher holds each paper so that all can see. Each
child reads his sentence to the class, and the class reads
each page in unison. The papers may be stapled with a
cover and title page listing each author, and the class-made
book put into the library collection for sustained silent
reading time.

This kind of activity continues, and within a few days
children are able to fold a sheet of paper into four and
record four frame sentences or more at one time. If the
individual responses are available on the chalkboard, then
the words are used to complete the frame. However, most
children are better able, at the beginning of grade one,
to draw a picture to complete the frame. As soon as any
letter has been taught and that letter-sound is in the
picture name, the teacher asks the child to say his answer
and to tell what letters he is saying. He then writes that
letter as part of his response. The teacher must demand
that children apply what has been taught; this judicious
nagging is part of the art of successful teaching.

Each child reads his written work to the teacher, and
the teacher reacts. The teacher's reaction to the child's
thoughts should, from the very beginning, be expressed
in writing. At the beginning of the year this written comment can be read to the child by the teacher; then gradu-

ally the teacher helps the child read the comment, helping less and less until the child is expected to read the comment without aid. This written comment should not be judgmental. Rather, it should reflect the teacher's sharing of the idea, e.g.

Your dog looks happy.

That is a big dog.

I like boats, too, George.

One of my favorite colors is blue.

I read a story about a dog that was lost. It was called *Lassie Come Home.*

Your cat must be a good pet for you.

I like that word "wonderful", etc.

This written reaction serves many important purposes:

1. It proves to the child that the teacher has read and understood what he has written.
2. It reinforces the understanding that written communication is important.
3. It pushes the child into reading writing other than his own.
4. It serves as a spelling help.

In their comments teachers should often use words that children have used but misspelled. This helps children to understand that they are *learning to spell,* that their spelling of words can be read and understood, but that it isn't perfect. We have seen many children read a comment by a teacher, then re-read their own writing and correct words that the teacher has modeled for them.

Another facet of this sharing period is equally important, but a much more difficult and sensitive task for the teacher. We have stated that creative writing is a child's recording of his own thoughts to the best of his abilities. It is very important that a teacher shares and reacts to a child's thoughts, but it is just as important that a teacher demands that a child practises to the best of his ability. This must be a sensitive demand. A teacher must not push a child beyond his capabilities, nor must she *always* require a child to do his very best. Children, as well as adults, have bad days. There are times when a child's lack of performance should be ignored. The teacher must know her children well, and respond sensitively and wisely to each child.

Usually, however, this sharing time would be the time when the teacher demands that each child use the spelling ability that he has. She demands that a child spells correctly words that he has the ability to spell or the "doozers" that are in a prominent place in the classroom.

This is also the time when a teacher sometimes tries to expand a child's story or thinking. The teacher's written comment can be in the form of a question to which the child is required to respond in writing:

What tricks can your dog do?

Where would you like to go on your boat?

Do you know any other stories about dogs?

Do you have any clothes or toys that are blue?

In this way, teachers are helping children expand both thinking and stories. When teachers request children to "write more" or "make their stories longer", the result is often a page of meaningless repetition, or a series of non-connected thoughts. The quality of a child's writing is much more important than the quantity. If a child is saying very little, he probably needs help in knowing what to say. A probing question will help him expand his writing in a meaningful manner.

Teachers have found it very valuable to set aside fifteen or twenty minutes at the end of each day to allow children to read their stories to the rest of the class. This procedure serves many purposes:

1. It provides additional reading practise for each student.
2. It demands that children listen to and comment on the thoughts of other children.
3. It provides the teacher with an opportunity to comment particularly on words or phrases that were used well by children or to create empathy and understanding within children by using one child's

experience as a basis for discussion, e.g., "Mary said she felt *proud* when her dog won first prize. Isn't that a good way to describe how she felt? Have you ever felt proud? When? Is it a good feeling? etc. Should we add the word 'proud' to our Interesting Word Chart?" or

"Bill plays ball with *his* friend. Do you play ball with your friends? What else do you do with your friends?"

4. It allows each child to feel pride in his accomplishments and in the accomplishments of his classmates, creating a fine feeling of rapport within the classroom.

Some children are reluctant at first to read their stories aloud. Many teachers solve this by asking the child's permission to read his story for him. As the teacher reads the child's story, she is careful to point out all the good things she possibly can about art work, thinking, or words. Gradually, the child is encouraged to stand beside the teacher as his work is shared, and to assist the teacher in the sharing by holding the work, reading parts, and showing illustrations, etc., until the child has gained enough confidence in his own ability to share work without assistance.

An outgrowth of this sharing period is a "class book". Teachers make a large, fancy book entitled *Our Wonderful Thoughts*. Each day, one or two children who have shared fine thoughts, or used particularly interesting words, etc., are invited to copy their work into a *Our Wonderful Thoughts* book, and to add their names to the author's column on the inside of the front cover. This book becomes an addition to the class library when it is filled and a new book is begun. Many teachers have dittoed off the material in *Our Wonderful Thoughts* books to send home as a classroom newspaper. This book has certainly been a motivating factor in increasing children's desire to write. Each child should have contributed at least once to each publication.

Thinking and Using Frame Sentences

Frame sentences are not used as an activity in and of themselves. They are used to record children's ideas. Themes or units of thought should provide the basis for much class or group discussion. The teacher then uses the language and thoughts to teach children to read and write. There is one caution in using frame sentences. Frames are used for drill and as a crutch to begin children writing. Not all children will need them, or want to use them. The use of frame sentences should decrease gradually as children become independent, and are filled with more colorful language. Overuse of frame sentences produces structured, stilted language.

Working with frame sentences is best done following total group discussion related to a theme. Work with children seated close to a large chalkboard so that their responses to questions can be written on the chalkboard, then read by children, and used for drill in as many ways as possible.

The following suggestions of simple frames have been used by children in working with the theme "Myself". Each frame should be developed individually.

I can _____ .	I see _____ .
I can't _____ .	I smell _____ .
I like _____ .	I hear _____ .
I have _____ .	I taste _____ .
I want _____ .	I feel _____ .
I play _____ .	I feel (emotions) _____ .
I can go _____ .	I can jump _____ .
I can run _____ .	I can ride _____ .
I can walk _____ .	I don't like _____ .
I can sit _____ .	I don't want _____ .
I can stand _____ .	I don't have _____ .
I can hide _____ .	Here is _____ .
A cat can _____ .	This is _____ .
Here are _____ .	There are _____ .

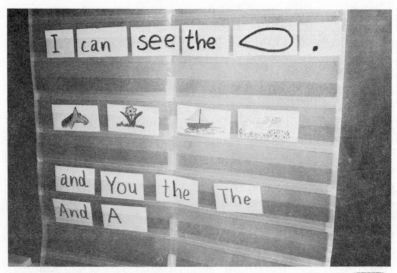

Frame sentences are developed as ways of reading and recording. The teacher and children work in the pocket chart, physically moving words to express different ideas. Children practise by placing different picture cards in the balloon, and by writing the sentences created on the chalkboard or on paper.

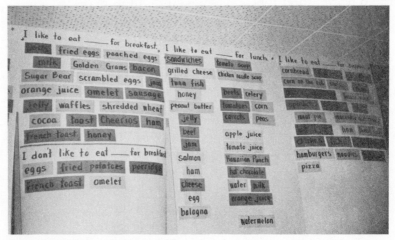

This recorded brainstorming about food made writing very simple in a grade one class.

Example Lesson Number One

Following a total group discussion where the teacher has brainstormed with all children for things they "can do", the majority of the class is supplied with 9″ × 12″ sheets of newsprint and assigned the task of recording something they "can do". The teacher teaches the children how to record through examples on the chalkboard, e.g., to record "I can ride a bike", children write the word "I" and illustrate the remainder of the thought.

While the majority of the class is recording in this manner, the teacher works in depth with a small group of six to ten children. The teacher asks each child what he "can do" and writes the responses on the chalkboard using each child's name in a frame:

Bill can play baseball.

Rose can skip.

Fiona can go to school.

Fred can play football.

Diane can bake a cake.

George can ride a bike.

Sylvia can play with her dolls.

Ted can watch T.V.

As each response is written on the chalkboard, *all* children chant each response. When all responses have been written, each child rereads his own response. Then children are requested to read each other's responses.

Teacher asks, "Where does it tell what Fiona can do? Who can read what Fiona can do? Who can find Bill's name? What can he do?"

Various word recognition drills can then take place:

1. Children can circle classmate's names as they are pronounced by the teacher.
2. Children can underline as many "cans" as possible.
3. As much phonics as has been taught can be practised, e.g., "Can you find a word beginning with F? Can you find a word that ends with F? Can you find a word with F in the middle? Can you find a big word? Can you find a little word?" etc.
   Always have children orally read the words they have found.
4. Sentence strips can be printed quickly using each child's sentence, e.g.,

Bill can play baseball.		Rose can skip.

These strips can be cut into words by the children, shuffled, and the sentences rebuilt. Then children trade sentence strips, telling their neighbors what the sentence should say as they pass their jumbled words to them. Each child checks his neighbor's work and listens to him read the sentence. The second or third time children do this activity, the teacher can leave them alone for a few minutes to circulate among the remainder of the class in order to expand their recordings or offer suggestions of other activities. To expand children's illustrations, questions should be asked, such as,

1. Where were you riding your bike?
2. What color was your sweater?
3. Was it sunny or was it raining?
4. What other things do you use to bake a cake?
5. Were there any other children with you?

Example Lesson Number Two

Another type of lesson is derived from discussing in depth what various parts of the body can do, i.e., feet, hands, eyes, ears, etc. The teacher discusses one aspect with the entire class, then allows children to practise a known frame in one of the ways suggested following the sample lessons, while she works with a small group of children.

As before, the teacher records children's responses on the chalkboard, but this time she substitutes the word "I" for each child's name.

The question "What can you do with your feet?" might elicit responses such as:

I can run.

I can walk.

I can hop.

I can skip.

I can jump.

I can dance.

I can pedal my bike.

I can kick.

As a child responds to the question, he is required to demonstrate physically that he *can* do what he is saying. As the teacher writes the sentences on the chalkboard, all children read each sentence. After all responses have been elicited and written, the teacher makes the children more aware of the written word by asking the following types of questions:

1. Are the sentences the same in any way? Where? How do they each begin?

2. Which sentence says, "I can pedal my bike?" "How do you know?" (number of words)

3. Which sentence says "I can hop?" "How do you know?" (length of word, hop, or phonetic clues) etc.

The teacher can then point to various sentences and allow individual children to prove they can read by pantomiming the action suggested. These sentences can then be written on sentence strips while the children watch, or as the children dictate the sentences to the teacher. The strips are distributed among the children, cut into words by the children and placed in a pocket chart. All children reread the sentences in the pocket chart. (They will probably be placed in a different order than they were on the chalkboard).

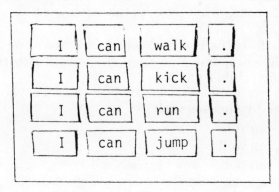

A simple excellent pocket chart may be made by taping two-inch strips of rigid vinyl, 0.15 to 0.20 mm thick, to an easel. The word cards are easily read through the clear plastic.

Example Lesson Number Three

Working with the sentences in the pocket chart provides another thinking-writing lesson. The teacher will need pictures and word cards for this lesson.

Begin by having the children reread the sentences in the pocket chart. Then remove all sentences but one, e.g., "I can walk." The teacher asks the question, "What else can walk?", and tries to have children respond in full sentences, e.g.,

A camel can walk.
A cat can walk.
A dog can walk.
A lion can walk.
A bird can walk.
A man can walk.
A lady can walk. etc.

Responses are placed on the chalkboard and reread. Children are asked to note how each sentence begins. The teacher points out that "A" sounds like a very short word, and so it is written with just one letter. "A" is underlined or circled by children in each sentence. Similarities in sentence structure are pointed out and "can" and "walk" are found in each sentence by children.

Children are then provided with picture cards and asked to sort these cards into two piles: those that "can walk" and those that "can't". (Allow discussion and argument between children. This can be done in a whisper — the noise level is up to the teacher.) While the children are doing this, the teacher makes certain that she has $\boxed{\text{A}}$ $\boxed{\text{can}}$ and $\boxed{\text{walk}}$ cards available for each child. Some $\boxed{\text{An}}$ cards are available or *An* may be written on the reverse side of the *A* card.

When children have completed their sorting, and the piles have been checked for accuracy by teacher and children together by chanting "A dinosaur can walk," or "A box can't walk," each child takes a picture from the "can walk" pile. Each child is then required to use his picture in an oral sentence,

A cow can walk.
A dog can walk.
A boy can walk. etc.

The teacher places all the $\boxed{\text{A}}$, $\boxed{\text{can}}$ and $\boxed{\text{walk}}$ word cards on the floor, along with cards containing periods $\boxed{.}$ (for those children who have already noticed that sentences end in periods). Children are asked to make sentences for their pictures using the word cards. Children build these sentences on the floor, read them, trade them, then place them in the pocket chart to be read in unison by the group., e.g.,

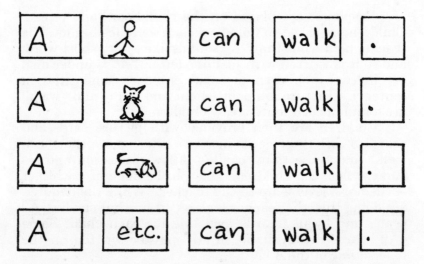

This pocket chart can be used by children throughout the day. Attach a large envelope with a clothespin. Children can substitute different pictures and drill themselves on the words.

Another lesson can be derived from using the "can't walk" pictures. By adding "t" to "can," the word "can't" can easily be taught, and children can form such sentences as

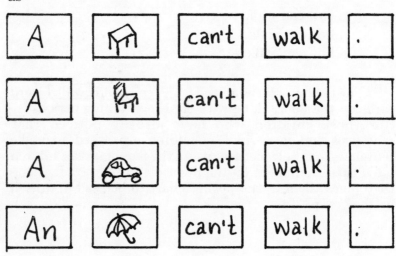

Example Lesson Number Four

Questions can be introduced by transformations of existing frame sentences:

Bill can walk.   becomes   Can Bill walk?

A camel can walk.   becomes   Can a camel walk?

To do this, the teacher will need to have the:

1. [A] card with a capital *A* on one side and a lower case *a* on the other,

2. [can] card with *Can* on one side and *can* on the other,

3. [·] card with a period on one side and a (?) question mark on the other.

The teacher should have the children practise by transforming the question into an answer. For beginning, the teacher should have two identical questions in the pocket chart:

The teacher makes certain that the pupils see that there are four words in each question plus a question mark, and the questions are identical.

The transformations are done only with the second line after the question has been answered orally. The first transformation is to shift the cards so that the second line reads [a] [camel] [Can] [walk] [?].

The second is to flip over the *a* and *can* cards so that the frame reads [A] [camel] [can] [walk] [?]. The teacher and children should read each transformed sentence as a declarative statement and the last transformation is to shift the [?] to a period [.]. With all of this the teacher may wish to add the word [yes] on a card to begin the second line.

This should be practised with many simple sentences, and then question strips, such as:

Can a dog run?

Can a kangaroo kick?   with envelopes pasted on

Can a bird fly?   the back of each

can be placed in the language center for individual work. In each envelope are the words, on separate cards, needed to answer the question. Later, children can be expected to copy the question on a sheet of paper and to transform the question into a full sentence answer.

Once children have gained reasonable facility with simple frames they should be able to move into two more difficult patterns. The teacher can use the more general form of question such as "What can walk?", "Who can run?" The teacher can ask questions that require a "no" answer such as "Can a camel fly?"

The children will discover they need "can't" and possibly "No" to build:

No, a camel can't fly.

The teacher should help the children to make *"can't"* by listening to *can* and *can't* and hearing the likenesses and the difference. The teacher should make *can* and *can't* while the children watch. No particular effort should be made to recognize *can't* as a contraction at this time unless a child notes the apostrophe and wonders about it or unless a child wants to say *cannot*.

Example Lesson Number Five

The most difficult words to learn are those that hold little meaning for children. The function or service words hold little meaning. Such words as *in, on, to, from, for, was, were, with,* etc., pose a greater problem for first graders than do *astronaut, boat, airplane, castle, princess,* etc.

To help children attach meaning to the service words, we suggest teaching them in frame sentences rather than isolated word drills. This is done by broadening the concept of the key word in each frame. Using the frame

"I can run"

discuss the word *run* with children, asking "Where do you run?" Children will respond with such frames as:

I can run to————————————.
I can run from ————————————.
I can run in————————————.
I can run on ————————————.
I can run over————————————.
I can run around ————————————.

"Do you always run by yourself?" will elicit "I can run with————————————."

Each frame is written on the chalkboard and read by the pupils, but much, much practise is needed for mastery of these service words. The next lesson would be devoted to building an understanding and use of one or two service words, e.g., "I can run to the store" could be reviewed. Then other endings for the frame "I can run to————————————" should be added.

"Do you run anywhere else?"

George can run to school.

Fred can run to the football field.

Sarah can run to her friend's house.

Sam can run to the corner.

Dave can run to Bill's house.

Maggie can run to the park.

Brad can run to Main Street.

These sentences need to be worked with. The children should underline or circle words; then cut sentence strips into words. They need to see that these small linking words which are often slurred in speech *are words* which look different and add different meanings to the verb.

The teacher needs to be alert to children's understanding of the small differences in meaning made by these words, and must provide much group and individual practise for children in using these words.

The difference between *running in* and *running on* needs to be dealt with.

I run in the park.   I run on the sand.
I run in the hall.   BUT   I run on the grass.
I run in the gym.   I run on the road.
I run in the backyard   I run on the sidewalk.

Other examples of frames to develop service words are:

1. Discussion of the word "like".
    I like a _____ .   I like the _____ .
    I like my _____ .   I like some_____ .
    I like to _____ .   I like lots of_____ .
                                                      etc.

2. Discussion of the word "play".
    I play with _____ .   I play a_____ .
    I play on _____ .   I play by _____ .
    I play in_____ .   I play behind _____ .
    I play at_____ .

3. Discussion of the word "jump".
    I can jump on_____ .   I can jump into _____ .
    I can jump in _____ .   I can jump across _____ .
    I can jump over _____ .   I can jump with_____ .

4. Discussion of the word "hide".
    I hide in _____ .   I hide inside _____ .
    I hide under _____ .   I hide over_____ .
    I hide beside _____ .   I hide with_____ .
    I hide behind _____ .   I hide on _____ .

5. Discussion of the word "walk".

I walk in _____ . I walk up _____ .
I walk on _____ . I walk down _____ .
I walk to _____ . I walk beside_____ .
I walk from_____ . I walk for_____ .
I walk with _____ . I walk from____to ____ .

Example Lesson Number Six

The teacher can read *There are Trolls*. The children and teacher can discern the frame sentences used in this book, and list them on sentence strips.

Trolls live in tree stumps
And live in old fridges.
There are trolls up the chimney
And some under bridges.

There are trolls that eat lemons
And some that eat snakes.
There's one (I've been told)
That gobbles up rakes.

Next the teacher can ask what could be substituted for *trolls* and the pupils and teacher could read the whole book together, in unison if the pupils have heard *There are Trolls* often enough, or as an echo book (the teacher reads a line, and the pupils repeat the line in unison), substituting dragons or elephants, etc., for trolls.

Next, a combination of four to six of the frame sentences could be used as a story frame to write about dogs, pets, children, etc. This "writing" should be done orally with the children before they write individually.

This kind of exercise is a step beyond simple frames and serves well to ready children to work with more sophisticated structures.

STORIES, POEMS, AND SONGS AS STRUCTURES

Stories, poems, and songs all have structures or patterns that pupils can recognize if they have worked orally often enough with individual pieces. Much of the recognition is intuitive or informal. The oral work in introducing a structure may be done in a single lesson, but usually it is a matter of several, perhaps twenty or more, oral workings with the story, poem, or song before the pattern will be freely used by most children.

We should recognize that there are a limited number of writing structures in common usage. If children work with six new structures each year to the point of mastery, and review these each year, they will have more than thirty ways of writing available to them as they enter secondary school. This is a reasonable goal, and it would mean that elementary pupils would be able to express themselves in writing in a literate, creative manner. Creativity grows from having enough skills and enough ideas to choose selectively.

We want to describe two sets of structures briefly, one story, one poem, and one song. The song, poem, and story are not related in theme. The first set is one that we have used extensively at the beginning primary levels and the second set we have used at the ending primary levels, although we have used both at all levels. A more detailed description of individual structures is given later as we talk about teaching from children's books, poems and songs. With each of these we presume that the teacher has used some form of hearing-seeing-and-using of the language orally, and that ideas have been brainstormed, discussed, evaluated, and classified.

Primary set number one

Story number one is the classic *Little Red Hen*. It lends itself to chanting, particularly the *not I* repeated sequences. The sequence is easily put onto a chart and lends itself to sentence strip and word card manipulation in the pocket chart. The story is easily dramatized.

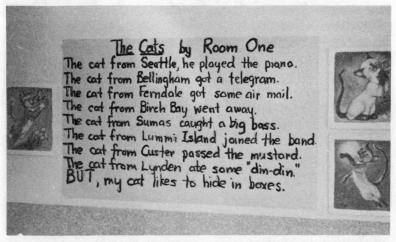

Story beginnings have been collected and posted high on the classroom wall.

The Cats by Room One

The cat from Seattle, he played the piano.
The cat from Bellingham got a telegram.
The cat from Ferndale got some air mail.
The cat from Birch Bay went away.
The cat from Sumas caught a big bass.
The cat from Lummi Island joined the band.
The cat from Custer passed the mustard.
The cat from Lynden ate some "din-din."
BUT, my cat likes to hide in boxes.

My Cat Likes to Hide in Boxes by Eve Sutton was the structure and inspiration for this grade two parody. They liked it so much that it was displayed in the hall outside their classroom.

Old tales with the repeated language recorded on word cards are used in grade
one to chant and sequence language.

After children have worked with *The Little Red Hen* orally and in the pocket chart, they can record their favorite memories, and attempt to record them in sequence. (Grade 1, November)

At Hallowe'en time this structure can be used by simply stating that old Mrs. Witch found a pumpkin seed one spring day and asked, "Who will help me plant the seed?" Of course, the characters shift to ghost and goblin and ghoul, etc. At Thanksgiving it can be the planting of a pumpkin and the baking of a pumpkin pie. At no special time, it could be the building of a swing or playground. These take-offs can be done orally first, and then in picture form, building the take-off directly on top of the original in the pocket chart. For some classes, this will be enough. For others, it will be possible to make the take-off into a class book, and still others will be able to make individual books of several versions.

Poem number one is *One, Two, Buckle My Shoe*. This is learned orally, and then take-offs can be written. (A kindergarten introduction of this poem can be found in detail on pages 83-88.) The take-off can fit the theme or season. Two kinds of words are needed to do this take-off. Children will need rhyming words for two, four, six, eight, and ten, and they will need words related to the theme. For example, the teacher might brainstorm for the characters, things or symbols of a holiday. This can result in the following kinds of verses:

> 1-2 ghosts saying boo,
> 3-4 witches at the door.

> 1-2 turkey in the stew
> 3-4 we all can eat some more.

> 1-2 a valentine for you,
> 3-4 guess who cards galore.

Again, these can be built orally, and children can then work with their versions as maturely as they are able.

Song number one, *The Farmer in The Dell,* is one of the easiest songs for children to work with. From brainstorming, the children can make and sing such verses as:

> The witch is in the air
> The witch is in the air
> Boo, boo she's scaring you
> The witch is in the air.

The turkey's in the oven
The turkey's in the oven
Yummy, yummy in my tummy
The turkey's in the oven.

One way of mechanically working with structures is to make scientific and remembered observations about each month or each season, and to record the information in song form. For example, in some areas the following are possible responses to September:

The leaves have fallen down.
The grass is turning brown.
The apples are getting ripe.
School has just begun.

Primary Set Number Two

No single story is used here, but rather a type of story. One of the simplest is the fairy tale. The teacher and children read several (more is better than less) fairy tales, and the teacher reads three or four favorites several times each. Next the children brainstorm (remember) for what makes a fairy tale a fairy tale, for beginnings, middles and ends. They will probably note the immediacy of the plot. After a beginning of *once upon a time in a far away place there lived a king and....* the problem of the plot is disclosed. Next we note the three-somes, the three poor brothers, the three guesses, the three something with success coming to the poorest, the youngest on the last try. And then the ending of happily ever after.

Children can work as a class brainstorming for possible middles and possible solutions, and then they can work individually or in small groups to create the tales. This can easily work into a project of book making or into creative drama.

Poem number two. No one poem is so well-known that we can merely mention the title and assume that it is as well known as *One, Two, Buckle My Shoe*. One poem that has almost instantaneous success is Margaret Wise Brown's *Bugs*. Obviously, if children have brainstormed

Margaret Wise Brown's poem "Bugs" is one of the best structures for children to use in recording their ideas.

for any content they can write many take-off versions. The original needs to be built on sentence strips, with word cards, or on a large sheet of paper. We have substituted pictures of bugs for the word "bugs" throughout so that the structure is blatantly apparent. From *Bugs* children have written as follows:

I like tracks
   Bear tracks
   Deer tracks
   Hare tracks
   queer tracks
   tracks on a fence
   tracks in the snow
   tracks on a rail
   tracks in a meadow

I like tracks
   thin tracks
   fat tracks
   dog tracks
   cat tracks
   black tracks
   white tracks
I like tracks

I like music
   good music
   bad music
   happy music
   sad music
I like music
   music on a sidewalk
   music on a street
   music with a rhythm
   music with a beat
I like music
   rock music
   roll music
   new music
   old music
   folk music
   baroque music
I like music
   by Peter Schalestock
   Age 8, Grade 3

Song number two. We have found that the song of the Chicago fire,

> One dark night, when we were all in bed,
> Old Mrs. O'Leary left a lantern in the shed.
> When the cow kicked it over, she winked her
>   eye and said,
> "There'll be a hot time in the old town tonight."

is a natural for take-off if we combine it with the structure of the Mother Goose rhyme, *Mrs. Mason bought a basin*:

> Mrs. Mason bought a basin,
> Mrs. Tyson said, What a nice 'un.
> What did it cost? said Mrs. Frost.
> Half a crown, said Mrs. Brown.
> Did it indeed, said Mrs. Reed,
> It did for certain, said Mrs. Burton.
> Then Mrs. Nix up to her tricks
> Threw the basin on the bricks.

Songs are made into song books by both teachers and children. Children work with the songs in sequencing them, and later with individual word cards.

Very quickly the teacher and children can write and sing #1 below and with a little help transform it into #2.

#1	#2
Ghost, ghost, ghost!	Ghost, ghost, ghost!
shouted Mrs. Post.	They scare us the most.
Ghoul, ghoul, ghoul!	Ghoul, ghoul, ghoul!
screamed Mrs. Pool.	Beware you silly fool.
Bat, bat, bat!	Bat, bat, bat!
yelled Mrs. Pratt.	Diving at your hat.
There'll be trick or treat	There'll be Hallowe'en
In the old town tonight!	In the schoolyard tonight!

Versions #1 and #2 lend themselves very nicely to a song book with one line boldly printed on the bottom or side of a page and an illustration of the line covering the rest of the page. Obviously, each book can be sung by the whole class as the author turns the pages and leads the singing.

USE OF NURSERY RHYMES

One, Two, Buckle My Shoe. The nursery rhyme is chanted until it is known orally. Cards are prepared as shown below and the poem is taught with the aid of a pocket chart.

Using well known language children work with the language in its written or pictured form. They learn to recognize some words, but more importantly they intuitively learn such concepts as *what is a word* and *left-to-right-progression*.

As the children chant the teacher should place the 1 and 2 in the chart, and the 3 and 4 as the children get to that part of the chant, continuing until the chant has been finished and all of the numerals are in place. The teacher then asks if the whole poem is represented in the chart. If the pupils say yes, the teacher should have the pupils chant again while she points to the 1 and then the 2 and then to the blank space that follows as they chant *buckle my shoe.* If the pupils say no, the teacher should ask what is missing. When it has been determined that *buckle my shoe* is missing, the teacher should hold up the three cards for *buckle, my* and *shoe* and ask which one is shoe and ask a child to place the picture of the shoe in the chart.

The children are then asked if the card is in the right place, and the first line chanted again while the teacher points to check if the word is in the proper place. Frequently the word will not be in the proper place, but the chanting usually will help the children determine where it belongs. The teacher may have to put it in place. The teacher then asks the children to determine what is missing and orally isolates *buckle* and *my.* Next she holds up the two cards and asks the children which is *buckle,* and then *my.* It is rare, when the whole class is working together, that some child doesn't respond correctly and give one of two reasons, *buckle* is longer or bigger, or *buckle* begins with a *b.* If the pupils do not notice the length, the teacher should tell them that *buckle* is longer to say by saying it with the children and comparing it orally with *my,* and then showing them that one is longer when written.

The teacher works through each line in a like manner, and the children then chant the whole poem again, this time alone, as the teacher points.

The teacher can now do several activities. There is no particular sequence for these.

1. She can have the pupils close their eyes and she removes or turns a card around, having the children try to read the chart silently and to shout (it will be noisy) the missing word.

2. She can remove two or three words, no more, and have the children replace the words.

3. She can remove eight to ten of the cards, one at a time, giving each card to a child and making sure that he can repeat the word represented, and then the children replace the words. The whole chart is then rechanted to check.

4. The teacher can say a word and have a child find it in the chart and then remove it, until about ten words are removed. The children who have removed a word then give the card to a different child to whom they teach the word and the words are replaced in the chart.

5. The teacher can give directions such as:

What word is under buckle?

What words are beside buckle?

What word is in front of buckle?

What word is below buckle?

What word is behind buckle?

What word is above shut?

to practise and teach the prepositions indicating location.

6. The teacher might prepare a ditto sheet leaving 3 to 6 spaces that children fill in.

7. The teacher should prepare a permanent chart with the poem printed as nearly as possible in the same way as the individual word cards. Children can then practise in the learning center by placing the word-cards on top of the poem itself.

8. The teacher should prepare sentence strips of each line of the same size as the large chart, and the strips can be placed in the learning center for pupils to put into sequence either directly on top of the chart or separately.

9. The teacher makes a small copy of the poem, and the pupils construct the poem by following the model using either the word-strips or the word-cards.

10. This nursery rhyme is a good pattern to copy in developing take-offs. A good way to practise using a pattern is to write seasonal take-offs so that pattern is reviewed and practised several times a year. For example, Hallowe'en can be done by brainstorming for all the symbols and figures of Hallowe'en. This will get witches, black cats, ghosts, goblins, bats, etc. The teacher may wish to brainstorm for rhyming words for two, four, six, eight and ten. The rhymes may come naturally without the brainstorming and listing. It is a natural step to suggest the 1-2 Buckle My Shoe rhyme be changed as follows:

1-2 (Hallowe'en word) (a phrase or word that rhymes)
Witches brew
Black cats mew
Pumpkins shine anew

3-4 Goblins at the door
Ghosts will soar
Vampires drink some more

A further variation can be made in a like way by suggesting that the children count beginning with zero.

0-1 The brew is overdone
Werewolves having fun
Children on the run

2-3 Ghosts don't scare me
Mummies floating free
Look out behind the tree

Similarly Christmas, Valentine's Day and Easter have sufficient ideas that the children have already experienced so they can create a class poem. Beginning lines might be:

1-2 Santa's got the flu	Valentines say guess who
Santa's in the flue	A red heart for you
Rudolph's feeling blue	Valentine, I love you

Don't have rabbit stew
An egg painted blue
Easter bunny's due

Children might use the 1-2 rhyme pattern to describe the seasons. We suggest brainstorming and direct observation with short walks outside to collect ideas and sensory impressions. With some classes it might be possible to do sufficient observation so that the take-off could be restricted to observation through the single sense of sight or hearing.

We hope that it will become obvious to teachers that children need lots of work physically manipulating language. Our experience indicates that some thirty to forty percent of children do not seem to understand how written language functions until they work with it physically through charts, sentence strips, and word cards. This is not just at kindergarten level, but something that needs doing throughout the primary grades. The teacher will need to make charts, sentence strips, and word cards for several books, poems, and songs. For books, the chart will be of a favorite page, the repeated portion such as *"Not I", said…,* or the beginning.

We use picture cards in most of our pocket chart work even though the children could and indeed do read the words represented without any difficulty. We do this for two main reasons: (1) The children have no difficulty with the words we can picture because they are the words that have the greatest meaning. (2) The pictures frequently recur in visual patterns that emphasize the structure of the written material. (Note the numerals, the words, and the pictures as a visual pattern in *"One, Two, Buckle My Shoe.")* (3) This reason is not overly important in one sense, but the stack of shuffled cards containing a few pictures can be immediately recognized by both teacher and children so that some housekeeping and sorting chores are easier to do.

We have found that the following nursery rhymes lend themselves to similar presentation and to brainstorming for ideas and take-off:

A Hunting We Will Go	(asking children what else they could catch and where would they put it.)
Polly Put The Kettle On	(asking children who else could do the putting, and then what else they could put on, and then what would they do if they put on certain items.)
Ladybug, Ladybug	(where the names and the hiding places vary.)
Baa, Baa, Black Sheep	(where the animal is changed as well as what the animal has, and children's names are substituted within the rhyme.)
Little Bo Peep	(numerous pages are made to show where the sheep might be.)

STRING LISTS AND STRING POETRY

Poetry can be sophisticated, but the beginnings of poetry should be fairly simple. Poetry is just saying something nicely about something.

Children can write poetry easily if they have:

1. ideas that are related to each other,
2. words to express the ideas,
3. some pattern or form,
4. the skill or the means to write the words.

We begin by writing the word *snow* on the chalkboard and drawing a line in front of it. We ask children what kind of snow they know. As they respond, we write their ideas in a list:

    white   snow
    fluffy
    cold
    drifting

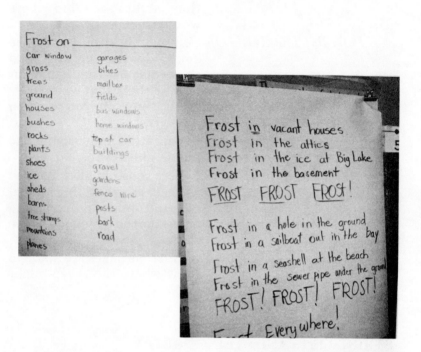

Frost on _____

Car window	garages
grass	bikes
trees	mailbox
ground	fields
houses	bus windows
bushes	home windows
rocks	top of car
plants	buildings
shoes	gravel
ice	gardens
sheds	fence wire
barns	posts
tree stumps	bark
mountains	road
planes	

Frost in vacant houses
Frost in the attics
Frost in the ice at Big Lake
Frost in the basement
FROST FROST FROST!

Frost in a hole in the ground
Frost in a sailboat out in the bay
Frost in a seashell at the beach
Frost in the sewer pipe under the ground
FROST! FROST! FROST!

Frost Everywhere!

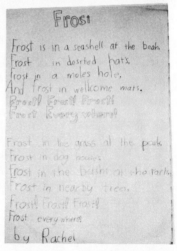

Frost

Frost is in a seashell at the beach
Frost in deserted hats,
Frost in a moles hole,
And frost in wellcome mats.
Frost! Frost! Frost!
Frost is everywhere!

Frost in the grass at the park,
Frost in dog houses,
Frost in the bushes at the park,
Frost in nearby trees,
Frost! Frost! Frost!
Frost everywhere!

by Rachel

One frosty morning the grade two class brainstormed for where they saw frost. As a class they wrote "Frost in vacant houses…," and then individual children created their own versions. They liked them so much that all the children copied their versions on chart paper and hung them in the room or in the hall.

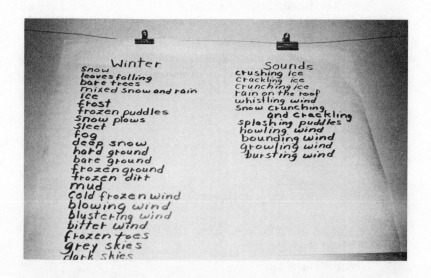

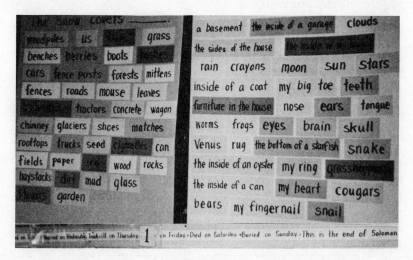

Each season provides a large number of ideas that may be recorded in classifications and used in numerous writing structures.

As each word is added the children chant:

> white snow
>
> white snow, fluffy snow
>
> cold snow, fluffy snow, white snow,

We brainstorm until we have forty words or more. More is better than less, and less than forty will mean that the exercise is unlikely to succeed.

We draw a blank after the word *snow* and brainstorm for what snow does, getting such words as:

> snow <u>falls</u>
>
> drifts
>
> blows
>
> flurries

Again we try to get forty or more words, and again we chant as we record.

We chant both lists, taking the first word from each list, and then the second:

> white snow falls
>
> fluffly snow drifts
>
> cold snow blows

Some combinations will make sense; some won't. We discuss or identify the nonsensical combinations. We chant and make more complex combinations chanting:

> white, fluffy snow falls and drifts
>
> cold, drifting snow blows and flurries
>
> etc.

We record (usually two or more children are assigned to this task while the teacher writes on the chalkboard) each of the words on a 3″ x 8″ word card. We give each group of 4-6 children four cards saying *snow* and eight words from each list. We ask them to make some phrases following the pattern:

> _____, _____ snow _____
>
> _____, _____ snow _____

We all read and share the results.

We switch to the pattern:

_____ snow _____ and _____ (the pupils need some *and* cards) and each group writes two or more sentences.

We brainstorm and make lists for:
1. where the snow falls
2. how the snow might fall
3. what they might do in the snow

These phrases are recorded and put onto phrase cards.

We ask the children to sort the words in each list, telling them to put them into two piles in any way that makes sense to them. We recommend that two or three sets of cards be made if this is to be done with the whole class. When the words are classified, the pupils who do not know how they were sorted guess the classifications. Eventually, we sort each list, put the words into some sequence, and affix each word or phrase card onto a long strip of masking tape. Finally, one child takes a long string and a yarn needle and sews each card into place by stitching through the masking tape. We hang the string lists, and now we have string lists from which children can create string poetry.

We have hinted about pattern or form. The blank-space phrases or sentences are a type of form. Any pattern that children already know, or any pattern that they can understand easily can serve as a guide for writing. We suggest free patterns rather than tightly structured patterns. We have in some of our other writings suggested haiku as a form. We have come to the conclusion that haiku is a sophisticated form, and that although children can follow it, we get better results when we use it only as a form that says something in ten to fifteen words. Haiku that has fifteen to twenty syllables (which of course is not haiku) is better for younger pupils because they concentrate upon thought, not form.

We use other patterns as follows:

I. tell how snow looks
   tell how it feels
   tell what you would do in it
                  or
   tell how and where it is falling
   tell how it looks when it first starts to fall
   tell how it looks after two hours
   tell how it looks the next day

II. We "Sing a song of six pence, pocketful of
    rye,..."

We have the whole song on a large chart; we sing, dance, or snap our fingers until we are sure everyone knows the song and feels its rhythm. We suggest that we sing a song of snowfall, or snowballs, or drifting snow, or snowmen, etc. We compose one or two take-off versions orally, record them on the chalkboard and sing them.

We use the pattern of 1, 2, buckle my shoe,

                  3, 4, shut the door.

writing:

1, 2, snow in my shoe, or the snow is blue, or the snowballs flew, etc.

We use the poem *Bugs* by Margaret Wise Brown as a pattern.

We use the poem *Is Anyone There?* by Mina Lewiton Simon as a pattern. We use as a pattern any poem or song that the children know or have learned previously.

III. We work with couplets or quatrains.

We build these in the pocket chart, shifting the words to demonstrate to children how words may be manipulated. We have the pupils manipulate the words with word cards. (The physical manipulation of the word cards seems necessary for many children if they are going to be able to respond freely when writing independently.) For example:

White snow snows.
Bright snow blows.

> Cold snow drifts.
> Powdery snow sifts.

is reorganized in the pocket chart to read merely

> White snow snows.
> Cold snow drifts.
> Bright snow blows.
> Powdery snow sifts.

We can reorganize by shifting the adjectives; we can reorganize by putting the word *snow* last in each line and asking the children to make the words make sense. We find that they quickly say:

> White, snowing snow.
> Cold, drifting snow.
> Bright, blowing snow.
> Powdery, sifting snow.

So we make cards with *ing* affixed, and perhaps another set with *ed* by suggesting that we make the snowstorm yesterday. This forces the children to work irregular verbs, and variations in word endings when adding affixes. The skills are taught because they are needed in a natural, easy way.

With all of these word strings we can turn the children to creating poetry in any one of their chosen forms. Each of the string lists is a poem in itself. From this oral input and the visual recording children can write easily. We get such poems as:

> I wish it would snow
> I would play in the snow,
>   lay in the snow,
>   jump in the snow,
>   go plump in the snow.
>
> I wish it would snow.

>   Drifting snow in the meadow
>   Sifting snow in the woods
>   Birds shaking and shivering,
>   Fluffing their feathers and
>   Searching for seeds on the
>   White weed stalks.

Is anyone there?
Is anyone there?
Out in the snow?
Shivering or shaking,
Quivering or quaking,
Burrowing or snuggling,
Sleeping or waiting,
While the snow falls gently on the bushes and
ground.

All this takes is a single word, a word for which children have lots of meaning, three or four hours of brainstorming over three or four days, lots of word cards, several
string lists, several patterns, and time for the children to
create.

CHAPTER V

Using Children's Books

There are hundreds of children's books that lend themselves to brainstorming, discussion and working with language. We will detail only four, and the teacher should be able to develop ways to work from her favorite books. Teachers should work from books that they genuinely like; children sense the teacher's love of literature, and it is one of the important messages that children discern.

We present the books here somewhat in ascending order, beginning with kindergarten and working to grade three. However, books have no proper level because books are about ideas and ideas have no grade levels. There are levels of maturity in the way in which a teacher presents materials, and levels of maturity of responses. Any idea worth discussing in kindergarten is worth discussing in grade two or three or at university level. If the idea is only worth discussing at one level, it is probably not important enough to waste primary school time on it.

Brown Bear

This book is a must for kindergarten classes. It is one of the most popular of beginning books with classes of young children. It has a distinct rhythm, a distinct structure, and a repeated rhyme. It is perhaps this coupling of the three features of poetry that makes the book a

Most old tales can be recorded in note form and the ideas classified according to character or time. Children work with the written language, classify it and chant it, and write in response to some portion of the story. This enables them to read several book versions of the tale.

favorite. Before the first reading has been completed orally, kindergarten classes are chanting *Brown Bear* freely. It lends itself to immediate extension, by merely adding animals, and it lends itself to extension by merely having the children use their own names:

Mary, Mary, whom do you see?   (whole class)
I see Billy looking at me.   (Mary alone)
Billy, Billy, whom do you see?   (whole class)
I see Harry looking at me.   (Billy alone)

It lends itself to extension whenever a group of nouns has been brainstormed:

Ghost, ghost, what do you see?
I see a witch looking at me.
Witch, witch, what do you see?
I see a bat looking at me.

We suggest the following patterned take-off as a poem children create and enjoy. Tell the children to imagine that they are a very little fish, hiding in the shadow of a rock and ask them what they can see. Brainstorm for five or six ideas and record these ideas pictorially on the chalkboard labelling each picture with the exact name given by the children.

Introduce orally the pattern:

Little fish, little fish,
What do you see?
I see a_____
But it didn't eat me.

and chant the six ideas from the chalkboard in the pattern orally.

Introduce the visual pattern in the pocket chart using a combined word and rebus pattern such as:

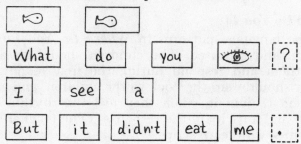

Transfer the chalkboard pictures to cards and insert each card into the blank and chant the poem again.

Brainstorm for thirty or more ideas and chant each one in the pattern. It may be desirable to come back to this another day adding ideas until forty or fifty have been provoked. Each of the ideas should be recorded on the chalkboard and each should be recorded on a card in pictorial form. If this is used late in the year, the words may be recorded on the reverse side of each picture card. Each child may draw and color his idea on a 3″ x 5″ card, and the cards strung on masking tape or a string so that the poem may be chanted from the "string" rebus.

Each child may draw and color (paint) his favorite idea on a sheet of paper. Each child should be encouraged to have little fish hiding somewhere in his picture. Each child can chant his picture with the teacher, and then during a group sharing each child can lead in teaching the class to chant from his picture. If the children are able, the teacher may have them label their drawings. Again, if the pupils are particularly interested or able, they can make a copy of the chant by copying from the pocket chart. The texts and the pictures can be compiled into a class book for repeated choral reading and individual reading in sustained silent reading.

The pupils and teacher may wish to provide an ending to the story. We have only one to suggest:

> Little fish, little fish,
> What do you see?
> I see a boy and girl
> And they did eat me.

Where Do You Live?

The language patterns in *Where Do You Live?* are common and repeated. The children should be able to sense them and respond during the first reading. The teacher should read the book to the children, and encourage them to join in when they feel the rhythm of the pattern and anticipate the responses. The teacher should make three word card strips,

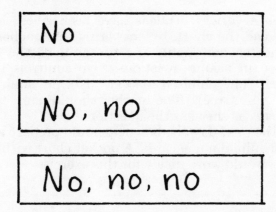

and point to each one several times as the children respond in unison.

The teacher and children should chant the book together. The teacher should point to one of the three no-strips as the reply.

The teacher and children should discuss the pictures, leading the children to understand that different animals live in trees, nests, caves, etc.

The teacher should draw the following pictures on the chalkboard,

and have the children orally classify animals from the book under these headings. The teacher should draw quickly each animal under the appropriate heading, or write its name, or both. The children will like even badly drawn pictures, and pictures will be necessary for some children to remember and respond. The children should brainstorm for ideas of other animals that live in a tree, cave, etc.

When a variety of ideas have been given, have the children read the chart, by answering the teacher's questions. The teacher should use the animals the children have given in asking questions. "Do squirrels live in a doghouse?" The children answer, "No, no, squirrels live in a_____(tree)." The teacher should point to one of the *no-strips* as she asks the question.

For the next day the teacher should prepare sentence cards and animal name cards. A pocket chart with individual words would work nicely for this exercise.

Do _____ live in caves?

No, no, _____ live in trees.

The animal name cards may be attached to the sentence cards with paper clips.

Do squirrels live in caves? No. no, _____ live in trees.

squirrels	pigs
bears	etc.

The teacher should read the top sentence, "Do squirrels live in caves?" The class may read the question with the teacher if they are able. The whole class and the teacher should repeat the question. One child is chosen to remove the word *squirrel* from the first sentence, and place it in the correct place on the bottom sentence. He then reads the sentence to the class, "No, no, squirrels live in trees." As one variation, other lines could be added,

No, no, _____ live in houses.

No, no, no, _____ live in caves.

The children would determine which answer fits. As another variation, the teacher should make sentence strips that leave the name of the abode blank. The pattern would be:

Do _____ live in caves?

Do _____ live in pens?

No, no, ____ live in ____.

No, no, ____ live in ____.

As a third variation the children could record their thought by mapping. The teacher draws on the chalkboard:

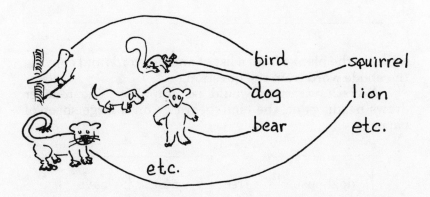

bird   squirrel

dog   lion

bear   etc.

etc.

One child draws a line from the animal to the correct home, and reads his map. e.g. "Bears live in caves." This same exercise may be repeated by using a ditto sheet.

A fourth variation would be to have the children fold a piece of paper into six squares

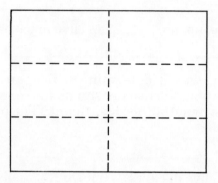

and draw an animal in each left hand square and its home in the right hand squares. These are then shared by reading, "_____ live in _____."

A fifth variation would be to have children copy the sentence strips,

Do ____ live in caves?		Do ____ live in trees?
No, no, ____ live in ____.	OR	No, no, ____ live in ____.

etc.

filling in the blanks from a list of animal words and copying the abode word from the question.

A sixth variation would be graphing. The teacher draws headings on the chalkboard or on a large sheet of paper;

doghouse	tree	nest	cave

From the animal list the children determine the abode and one child draws as many circles as needed under each heading to represent the number of animals living in each type of dwelling.

The findings can be recorded both mathematically and in words as the children read:

_____ animals live in trees

_____ animals live in nests.

The teacher should use *Where Do You Live?* to develop the concept of animal foods.

The teacher should note with the children that the dog in the illustration is eating from the dish. The teacher should ask and then brainstorm for what might be in the dish. Brainstorm for what monkeys eat, what birds eat, pigs eat, bears eat, etc. The teacher should have pictures ready of things animals eat (meat, bones, bananas, apples, hay, bark, leaves, insects, pollen, worms, bugs, grass, thistles, fish, etc.). The teacher should tape these pictures to the chalkboard near the top and under each picture draw and label the animals the children think would eat the pictured food, e.g.,

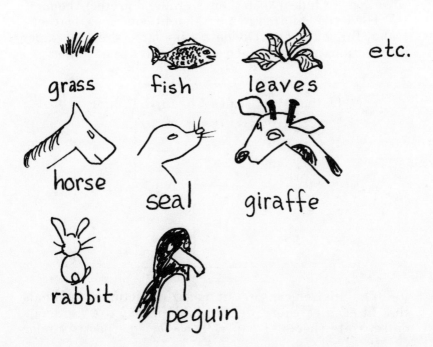

Through discussion, the teacher should lead the children to recognize that some animals fit more than one category.

The teacher can lead the children to read the chart several ways using the following sentence patterns:

(number)   animals eat grass.

_____   animals eat fish.

(animal name)_____, _____, and _____ eat grass.

(animal name) eat (foods), _____, and _____.

The teacher should use *Where Do You Live?* to develop the concept of how animals keep warm. The teacher should review the fact that some animals eat the same things, and some do not. She should review that their homes are also different. The teacher should ask, "Why do animals have homes?" and keep the discussion going until the children volunteer the idea that animal coverings (or hides) keep them warm and protect them.

Have the children name different coverings, feathers, scales, fur, hide, etc. Divide a very large sheet of paper into sections and label each section with one covering.

feathers	scales	fur	hide

The children can cut out magazine pictures of animals that fit each category, or the children may draw animals on separate sheets of paper. These can be pasted under the proper heading. The chart may be used as a room mural and read as other charts have been read. In the morning during attendance, the teacher could say, "Good morning, Mary, do you have on a dress today?" Mary would answer, "Yes, but horses have hides," (choosing something from the chart).

This same idea may be transferred to book form in this way:

On the first page the child could draw something he or she is wearing, and with help if necessary, print the word on the blank. On the next page he would again choose an animal and draw it, printing the correct words on the blanks. This can be done as a class book, with each child doing one page. Or each child could make his own book and then take it home. Whichever way this is done, each child should be given the opportunity to share his ideas with the class.

The children could make a different "Feel Book" in the following manner. They would use the same vocabulary as used in *Where Do You Live?* and reverse the idea of the child's book that asked, "Do you have on a shirt? e.g.

The scales can be made by glueing macaroni (shell type) on the drawing of a fish.

Feathers can be gotten somewhere. Fishing tackle stores have feathers for tying flies.

Dried coffee grounds make a good "fur" looking appearance.

A visit to a zoo would give the children a good view of the different kinds of animals they have been discussing. Upon their return from the zoo, the children could draw the number of fur bearing animals, the number with hides, etc. that they saw. This in turn could be put in the form of a graph:

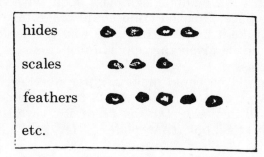

This idea could lead the children to other areas, classifying animals by:

1. How they move (gallop, run, swim, etc.)
2. Big and little animals
3. Sounds that animals make
4. Vegetarian and carnivorous
5. Domestic and wild
6. Where they are found, etc.

The Boy Who Never Listened

Concepts
1. Loud and louder.

Recall with the children the noises Teeny Tom made. Challenge the pupils to recall these in sequence.

talked
snored
laughed   Elicit as much of the spelling from
whistled   the children as has been taught.
sang
screamed
cried

Challenge the pupils to rank order the noises Teeny Tom made from least noisy to noisiest. This should elicit much imitative noise-making if circumstances permit it. Two children may be designated to be Teeny Tom while the rest listen. Teeny Tom #1 talks while Teeny Tom #2 snores, then Teeny Tom #1 and #2 change noises. The class decides whether snoring or talking is louder. One child may take both parts alternately while the rest listen. Various pairings are made while determining degrees of loudness.

The teacher may wish to have one child talk, snore, laugh, etc. as loudly as he can while a tape recorder is recording with a microphone some distance from the noise maker. The contrast in loudness as recorded may be more distinguishable.

The teacher may wish to develop language frames to record the loudness:

John's _____ is louder than his _____ .

or

John's _____ is loud but his _____ is louder.

Recall the sounds drowned out by the seven noises made by Teeny Tom and rank order them for loudness. Compare the two lists and challenge the pupils to explain why the pairings of the rank order are the same or different than the pairings within the story.

The teacher may wish to use the language frame:

A _____ is louder than a _____ but a _____ is loudest of all.

The children would use any three of the listed drowned out sounds to fill in the frame. The children could brainstorm for the loudest sound in the world to fill in the third blank.

The teacher should discuss loudness of sounds by asking children when a schoolbell is loud and when it might be hard to hear, when an airplane motor is loud and when it might be hard to hear. She should discuss several noises in this way and then extend the ranking scheme to include the notion of equal proximity of ear and noise origin.

She might work with the language frame:

An airplane motor is louder than a school bell ringing unless _____ .

There are numerous possible answers that should be brainstormed. The two noun phrases should be erased leaving the frame:

_____ is louder than _____

unless _____ .

Answers for this frame should be brainstormed and discussed until numerous noises have been discussed beyond those in the book. Each child then might work independently to complete one picture and one sentence to illustrate his favorite noises. These could be built into an *Our Favorite Noise Book*.

2. Sounds of the City.

Reread pages 34-37 orally. Locate Teeny Tom and his mother in the city and then listen as if you were there. Brainstorm for sounds, "all kinds of sounds." Note the four sound classifications in the story: sad, happy, soft and loud. Use these as a chalkboard heading or pocket chart headings and classify the sounds.

Suggestions: (a) Take a quiet walk with a tape recorder with the children to a city corner.

(b) Tape a similar corner's sounds without the children.

(c) Look at many books for city street scenes as photographed or illustrated. Imagine the noises to be heard.

(d) Record noises from one or more T.V. shows.

Use any or all four suggestions to elicit sounds for classification.

The teacher may use these sound-word classifications to build a poem or a poetic prose statement or statements.

The happy sounds of _____ .

_____ .

_____ .

The sad sounds of _____ .

_____ .

_____ .

The soft sounds of _____ .

_____ .

_____ .

The loud sounds of _____ .

_____ .

_____ .

The teacher might do the same activity for the country, the forest, the zoo, or the seashore.

3. Noise and Noise Pollution.

Some noises may be thought of as inevitable because we want to do something — the starting of a car motor — but one that could be eliminated or controlled. Some noises could be thought of as out of our control, the noise of thunder, rain, or a waterfall. Some noises might be thought of as giving messages that help us survive, the telephone ringing or a referee's whistle.

Brainstorm for noises and classify them. Challenge the children to make the world quieter by suggesting less noisy substitutes for the noises they think of.

Brainstorm for whistles, or sirens, or bells or buzzes that give messages. List the noises and the messages such as:

> Doorbells that tell us someone's at the door.
> Telephone bells that tell us someone's calling.
> Dinner bells that tell us lunch is ready.

Have the children look for melodious patterns of expression and possible rearrangements of lines to form stanzas. Consider and practise chanting in two parts.

Part one	Part two
door bell ringing	someone's at the door
telephone bell ringing	someone's calling on the phone
dinner bell ringing	lunch is ready
etc.	

OR

make the noise	someone's at the door
or use onomatopoeia	
ding a ling ling ling	
ring a ring a ling	
ding ding ding, etc.	

OR

interchange so that part two comes first. When the parts have been learned then the sequence of the parts can be varied so that one person or one team makes a noise and the others try to give the correct response.

Expanding from the language of the book,

1. Reread orally page 60. Brainstorm as necessary for soft, loud, high, low, sharp, and dull sounds, depending upon how much sound classification has been done recently.

Expand the sentences as follows using any of the appropriate sounds:

He liked the soft sounds...expanded to

He liked the soft sounds *of rain falling*

or *of snow fluttering*

or *of bird's wings flapping,*

etc.

This could easily lead to a child making his own *Sounds I Like* book of six or more pages:

Page 1   I like the soft sounds of _____.

Page 2   I like the loud sounds of_____.

Page 3   I like the high sounds of_____.

Page 4   I like the low sounds of _____.

Page 5   I like the sharp sounds of_____.

Page 6   I like the dull sounds of _____.

2. Classify sounds by the ways we express them. For example, pages 55, 56, 57, 58 and 59 all say "the roar of_____." What else roars? Page 47 has a horn blare. What else blares? Page 46 uses *groan,* etc. Brainstorm for noises that sing, hum, undulate, screech, whisper, murmer, etc. Any of these might be arranged into poems or poetic prose.

Couplets might be made such as:

Birds sing	People talk	Lions roar
Bells ring	Parrots squawk	Lamas snore

The Judge

We have used *The Judge* in grades two through eight. The presentation is essentially the same at all grade levels; the difference comes in the responses of the children.

We begin by writing the title on the chalkboard and allow the class to solve what is written. We ask what a

judge does and try to elicit responses that center about
hearing evidence and making decisions. With some groups
we write the word *prejudge* and then *prejudice* to develop
the original meaning of the word, to decide without
evidence. We ask where a judge works and elicit the words
court and *courtroom* and record them on the chalkboard.
We tell the pupils that in this story there is a (using chalk)
courtroom an... (and we wait a few seconds. If we get
no response we add another letter *ann,* wait, and then
announ, and finally *cer,* with another wait.) We discuss
announcers and ask what a courtroom announcer might
announce. We elicit responses, and finally get or elicit by
writing that he will announce *pr*_____, *pris*_____,
*prison*__, *prisoners.*

We now play all the parts and read the story orally;
We read as the courtroom announcer:
> This is prisoner number one.
> Let justice be done!

We read as prisoner number one:
> Please let me go, Judge.
> I didn't know, Judge,
> That what I did was against the law.
> I just said what I saw.

We now let our chalk do the communicating and we
write quickly (if you do not write quickly you will lose
your audience) and clearly:
> A horrible thing is coming this way,
> Creeping closer day by day.
> Its eyes are scary
> Its tail is hairy

And then we say orally the next line:
> I tell you, Judge, we all better pray!

We discuss how this should be chanted. Most often
we decide that the first line needs power and fairly quick
speed with special volume and emphasis on the word
horrible. The second line is whispered to emulate creeping,
and *scary* (we sometimes write this with a shaking hand)
tremulously. We practise this first part two or three times

to develop the quality that we want. As may be obvious, no help is given by the teacher while she is writing, and the children struggle their way through the message helping each other.

We now play the judge and sentence the prisoner with a rhyming couplet.

The Judge is a cumulative story, the courtroom announcer now announces prisoner number two, prisoner number two repeats what prisoner number one said and adds a couplet describing the monster, and the judge sentences prisoner number two. We write what prisoner number two adds on the chalkboard and we all chant together. We do this for prisoner numbers three, four, and five, and finally close the book in the middle and ask the pupils how the story ends. The story is told in pictures, and the plot is obvious to most classes, the monster comes and eats the judge and the prisoners go free.

There are several activities that the pupils can now do to work with the language. This story is better than many stories in that there are many activities which flow naturally from it. This list can serve as a guide to the kinds of activities that might be done following other stories:

1. Pupils can predict the ending. This story is not really a good one for predicting, because once one child has suggested that the monster comes and eats the judge everyone agrees that that is the ending, so there is not much discussion.

2. Pupils can draw the monster, or create it with some other art media. To do so requires that they pay attention to the details given in the story. If the pictures of the book have already been seen, this is not a particularly good activity. As stated elsewhere, we recommend that stories be read without showing pictures, at least during the first reading.

3. The pupils will note the pattern of each prisoner adding a couplet, being introduced by a couplet, and being sentenced by a couplet. Pupils, or small groups of pupils, can be assigned to be prisoner number 6, 7, 8, 9 (we have

done as many as thirty-four), and each new prisoner must add a couplet describing the monster. Later they may write announcing couplets and sentencing couplets. We suggest that for grades two and three the teacher compose three or four sample couplets with the whole class before setting the pupils to work independently.

One activity after the additional couplets have been written is to check them for contradictions. If a class writes ten or more couplets simultaneously, couplets may be written which contradict each other. This requires some editing and rewriting.

4. The original version or the class augmented version is marvelous for dramatization with a chorus that chants the part that is being repeated.

5. Several classes, after hearing this book, have asked if they could rewrite the story from memory. We normally would caution against doing this, but *The Judge* has such powerful language that the pupils have genuinely enjoyed it. The results have been a marvelous mixture of pupil and Zemach language.

6. The book goes into the library corner and is used in SSR.

7. The teacher may tell the pupils that this is a cumulative story, and pupils may search the library for other stories of this type. These are all then shared orally in class.

8. The pupils may set to writing their own cumulative stories. These may follow the pattern of *The Judge* or merely be cumulative in style. Any of these could' then be done dramatically.

9. The original description that was on the chalkboard is put on chart paper and hung where it can be chanted when there is a free moment. The augmentations created by the pupils may be added.

10. *The Judge* may begin theme work on dragons, monsters, and the like.

11. The content of *The Judge* can be set to song. It will easily fit into *The Farmer in the Dell*. For example,

The judge is in the court.

Here comes prisoner number one.

etc.

12. The pupils can brainstorm for monster movements, and these can be worked on in P.E. or in the classroom if space permits.

13. The monster can be given a name. Pupils can examine the names of monsters that they know, and they may wish to use the *saurus* (terrible lizard) and *pter* (flying) from Greek to make' very scientific sounding names.

14. The pupils can look for other books by Harve and Margot Zemach.

15. The lines of *The Judge* can be put on sentence strips, and pupils can sort these into various sequences for chanting.

16. The individual words and the punctuation marks can be put onto cards. Children can rewrite *The Judge* by sorting and manipulating the cards into sequence. Many second grade children, and some third grade children, need this kind of practise. Reluctant readers need this particularly.

The Judge may be the basis for the language program for as long as two months. If so, it becomes the remedial reading program, because every child in the class will know the original so well that they now can practise with a book until the words on the page become fixed in the brain, and the various activities growing from the book give the poor reader an opportunity to learn how language functions.

CHAPTER VI

Themes

Themes are about ideas; themes are ways of developing concepts; themes are thoughts, examined and re-examined; themes are nebulous and somewhat difficult to describe.

Teaching through a theme is very similar to teaching through a unit; teaching units have been used for many years and are excellent. In fact, a unit may turn into a theme. The distinction between a theme and a unit is mostly in the doing. A unit has a planned beginning, middle, and ending; the theme has only a beginning, a planned beginning to stimulate exploration. A theme requires planning and replanning to reach its middle and ending; this is done after the inception and acceptance of the theme by the children.

An educational theme is akin to a musical theme. In a musical theme the same notes recur in different rhythms, keys, forms, and cadences; the theme holds together a series of otherwise unrelated musical expressions. A fully explored theme has many variations. As a composer works with a theme he explores hundreds of variations that may never appear in the finished score. So it is with the educational theme. With an educational theme the exploration takes place within the classroom as the teacher and pupils work together. Just as a composer doesn't know exactly what variations will emerge and what will be the finished

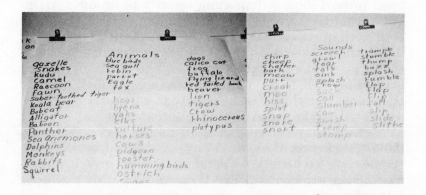

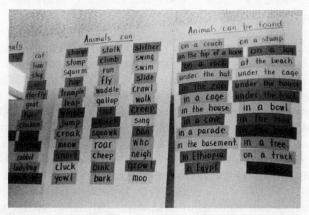

Brainstorming as part of an animal theme in grade three resulted in lots of ideas being recorded for chanting, classification, and reference. The initial recording was done on the chalkboard.

score, the teacher does not know exactly what activities will be used to develop the theme nor what the culminating activity or product will be. These emerge as the theme is explored.

Just as a composer may explore for hours to produce seven minutes of music, the teacher and pupils may explore for days before they select the final variations to be practised toward some culminating activity or product. Without trying to subtract from the importance of the skills employed in creating the variations, the crucial ingredient is the theme. Without the theme there can be no variations, no exploration of thought. The skills needed to explore an idea, to examine a theme, are acquired through the doing. The theme is the glue that integrates otherwise unrelated, irrelevant skills and practise drills.

Themes are special but their names may seem mundane. Teachers and children have worked successfully on themes labeled *beauty, mapmaking, words, myself, happiness, space exploration, The Wizard of Oz, fish, pioneers, folk tales,* etc. There are literary themes; there are social study themes; there are science themes; there are interdisciplinary themes. The naming does not do much to explicate.

Themes come from the teacher through her ability to select and generate interest. The theme of *Rudyard Kipling* which resulted in the delightful Just-So story *How the Skunk Got His Smell* was teacher generated through months of oral reading and discussion. (See RIOTT pp. 81-85). Themes come to school inside of children. These themes emerge as the teacher discovers pupils' interests and nurtures them. The theme *Myself* (see RIOTT pp. 31-36) is an example of a theme that comes to schools largely within each child. *The Wizard of Oz* was a combination of teacher input and what pupils already possessed through the teacher's oral reading of Baum's book and the children's having seen the classic movie version.

The development of themes is the heart of a language program. Thoughts and the development of thoughts must be perceived by the children as the reason for language (or content area) lessons. This requires that the teacher teaches seriously and that the teacher responds seriously to the ideas of children. This is serious responding, not necessarily serious ideas. We have worked delightfully, and with much laughter, with the theme of food and eating. Children sense great joy and satisfaction from working seriously and achieving.

One of the difficult jobs in teaching is the art of making the learning of skills easy enough so that the children almost always focus upon meanings rather than upon skill tasks. As adults, most of us write or talk without consciously thinking of the process. This is our goal for children. Children will need to focus upon spelling as they learn to write, but they should never get so concerned about spelling that they forget what they are trying to say. The skills and the learning of skills must remain subservient to the thoughts.

Many of the activities in this book might be described as ways of working with language that children enjoy or have fun in doing. However, having fun while doing an exercise is not sufficient reason for doing an exercise. The exercises must emerge from serious inquiry if children are to learn how to think and be able to transfer their learnings to non-exercise situations. The spelling bee has always been a time that children enjoyed, but it does no more to teach spelling than writing words five times each from the weekly list.

The spelling bee is likely to be fun, and the writing of words five times is likely not to be. Neither focuses upon thinking or serious thought. The focus is upon skill. Most children become skillful when we concentrate on skill, so we tend to conclude that there is something wrong with those children who do not respond to skill teaching. We should consider that some children cannot understand what they are supposed to be learning, and cannot make themselves learn skills for skills' sake. It is for the non-learner or poor learners particularly that the emphasis upon ideas is important. It is through the concentration upon ideas that they realize what they need to learn in language, and then practise until they learn.

Bibliography

BAUM, FRANK L. *The Wizard of Oz*. New York: Reilly & Lee.

BROWN, MARGARET WISE. "Bugs," *The Fish with the Deep-Sea Smile*. New York: E. P. Dutton & Co. 1938.

GREEN, JOHN. *There Are Trolls*. Winnipeg, Canada: Peguis Publishers Limited, 1974.

GROVER, E. O., editor. *Mother Goose, the Classic Volland Edition*. Northbrook, Ill.: Hubbard Press, 1971.

KIPLING, RUDYARD. *Just So Stories*.

LEWIS, KATHERINE. *The Purple Snail*. Happiness Is Reading Series. San Rafael, California: Leswing Press, 1969.

MCCRACKEN, ROBERT A. AND MARLENE J. *Reading Is Only the Tiger's Tail*. San Rafael, California: Leswing Press, 1972.

MCCRACKEN, ROBERT A. AND MARLENE J. *How Do You Say Hello to a Ghost? This is the House that Bjorn Built. Where Do You Live?* et. al. Tiger Cub Readers. San Rafael, California: Leswing Press: 1973, 1976.

MACHADO, JOAN. *Almost Just Alike*. Happiness Is Reading Series. San Rafael, California: Leswing Press, 1970.

MARTIN, BILL, JR. *Brown Bear*. New York and Toronto: Holt, Rinehart and Winston, 1970.

POHLMANN, LILLIAN. *The Bethlehem Mouse*. Happiness Is Reading Series. San Rafael, California: Leswing Press, 1970.

RANDALL, FLORENCE. *The Boy Who Never Listened*. Happiness Is Reading Series. San Rafael, California: Leswing Press, 1969.

SIMON, MINA LEWITON. *Is Anyone There?* New York: Atheneum, 1967; Toronto: McClelland and Stewart, 1967.

ZEMACH, HARVE AND MARGOT. *The Judge*. New York: Farrar, Straus and Giroux, 1969; Toronto: Doubleday Canada Ltd., 1969.

Index